Intimate Death

Intimate Death

How the Dying Teach Us
How to Live

❖

MARIE DE HENNEZEL

translated by

CAROL BROWN JANEWAY

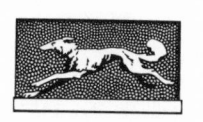

ALFRED A. KNOPF   NEW YORK   1997

THIS IS A BORZOI BOOK
PUBLISHED BY ALFRED A. KNOPF, INC.

Library of Congress Cataloging-in-Publication Data
Hennezel, Marie de.
[Mort intime. English]
Intimate death : how the dying teach us how to live /
by Marie de Hennezel ; translated by Carol Brown Janeway.
—1st American ed.
p. cm.
ISBN 0-679-45056-4 (hc). —ISBN 0-679-76859-9 (pbk.)
1. Death—Psychological aspects. 2. Terminally ill—
Psychology. 3. Hennezel, Marie de. I. Title.
BF789.D4H42413 1997
155.9'37—dc20 96-32774 CIP

Manufactured in the United States of America
First American Edition

to Laure, Édouard, and Jean

◇ ◇ ◇ ◇ ◇ ◇ ◇ ◇ ◇ ◇ ◇ ◇ ◇ ◇ ◇ ◇ ◇

Foreword

HOW DO we learn to die?

We live in a world that panics at this question and turns away. Other civilizations before ours looked squarely at death. They mapped the passage for both the community and the individual. They infused the fulfillment of destiny with a richness of meaning. Never perhaps have our relations with death been as barren as they are in this modern spiritual desert, in which our rush to a mere existence carries us past all sense of mystery. We do not even know that we are parching the essence of life of one of its wellsprings.

This book is a lesson in living. The light it casts is more intense than that of many philosophical treatises; it does not offer thought but, rather, bears witness to the most profound of all human experiences. Its power derives from facts and from the simple way these are represented. *Represented* is exact—"to render present again" that which escapes our awareness: the far side of things and of time, the heart of anguish and of hope, the suffering of another, the eternal dialogue between life and death.

It is this dialogue that re-presents itself in these pages, the dialogue that Marie de Hennezel sustains unbrokenly with her dying patients.

I WILL never forget the visit I made to the palliative care unit to which she was currently devoting her energies. I was aware of her work, and we had talked about it from time to time. I was immediately struck by the sense both of strength and of gentleness in her words, a sense I had again when I met the doctors and nurses on her team. They talked to me about their passion, their efforts, government delays, the hurdles still to be overcome. Then they took me to the bedsides of the dying. What was the secret of these men's and women's serenity?

What was the source of the peace in their eyes? Each face imprinted itself on my memory like the face of eternity itself.

It is Danièle's I see again, perhaps because of her youth and her silence. Paralyzed, unable to speak, she could communicate only by blinking her eyelids or using the one finger she could still move to tap at letters on a computer screen. And yet, despite this utter helplessness, she was full of life, full of curiosity about the other side, which she was about to enter without the help of religious faith.

Marie de Hennezel tells us about the dignity of Danièle's last moments and those of her companions in sickness; she also tells us modestly but therefore all the more movingly about the unwavering supportiveness of the teams who accompany them on their last journey. She lets us experience the everyday adventure of the discovery of another human being, the engaging of love and compassion, the courage in the gentle movements that tend these damaged bodies. She shows how it is the love of life, not any death wish, that feeds the choices they make and the things they do.

We have talked about these matters often. I asked her question after question about the sources of the power that erases anguish and brings peace, and about the extraordinary transformations she sometimes witnesses in people who are about to die.

At the moment of utter solitude, when the body breaks down on the edge of infinity, a separate time begins to run that cannot be measured in any normal way. In the course of several days sometimes, with the help of another presence that allows despair and pain to declare themselves, the dying seize hold of their lives, take possession of them, unlock their truth. They discover the freedom of being true to themselves. It is as if, at the very culmination, everything managed to come free of the jumble of inner pains and illusions that prevent us from belonging to ourselves. The mystery of existence and death is not solved, but it is fully experienced.

That is perhaps the most beautiful lesson of this book: Death can cause a human being to become what he or she was called to become; it can be, in the fullest sense of the word, an *accomplishment*.

And then, is there not some fragment of eternity in humankind, something that death brings into the world, gives birth to? From the paralysis of her hospital bed, Danièle has a last message for us: "I don't believe in a God of justice, or a God of love. It's too human to be possible. What a lack of imagination! But nor do I believe that we can just be reduced to some bundle of atoms. Whatever tells us that there's something beyond matter—call it soul, or spirit, or consciousness, whatever you prefer—I believe in the immortality of *that*. Reincarnation or arriving at an entirely new plane of being—it's discovery by death!"

It's all there, in these few words: the body dominated by the spirit, terror conquered by confidence, the fullness of an achieved destiny.

True to Danièle, Marie de Hennezel's work is dense with humanity.

How do we learn to die?

If there is an answer, few accounts can provide it with so strong an inspiration as this one.

François Mitterrand

◇ ◇ ◇ ◇ ◇ ◇ ◇ ◇ ◇ ◇ ◇ ◇ ◇ ◇ ◇ ◇ ◇

Preface

WE HIDE death as if it were shameful and dirty. We see in it only horror, meaninglessness, useless struggle and suffering, an intolerable scandal, whereas it is our life's culmination, its crowning moment, and what gives it both sense and worth.

It is nevertheless an immense mystery, a great question mark that we carry in our very marrow.

I KNOW that I will die one day, although I don't know how, or when. There's a place deep inside me where I know this. I know I'll have to leave the people I love, unless, of course, they leave me first.

This deepest, most private awareness is, paradoxically, what binds me to every other human being. It's why everyman's death touches me. It allows me to penetrate to the heart of the only true question: So what does my life mean?

Those who are privileged to accompany someone in life's final moments know that they are entering the most intimate of times. Before dying, the person will try to leave his or her essence with those who re-main—a gesture, a word, sometimes just a look to convey what really counts and what thus far has been left—either from inability or inarticulacy—unsaid.

Death, which we will live to the end one day, which will strike our loved ones and our friends, is perhaps what pushes us not to be content with living on the surface of things and people, pushes us to enter into the heart and depth of them.

AFTER YEARS of accompanying people through the living of their final moments, I do not know any more about death itself, but my trust in life has only in-creased. I am certain that I live more intensely and more awarely those joys and sorrows that I am given to live, and also all the little, daily, automatic things—like the simple fact of breathing or walking.

I may also have become more attentive to the peo-ple around me, aware that I will not always have them at my side, longing to explore them and to contribute as much as I can to what they are becoming and what they are called to become.

Moreover, after spending years with what are called "the dying," although they are in every way "the living" until the very end, my own sense of aliveness is more intense than ever. I owe this to those I have imagined myself to be accompanying, but who, in the humility of their suffering, have revealed them-selves as masters.

WE ALL TRY to see through death. Is there some-thing on the other side? When people leave us, where do they go? It's a question that causes great pain—that is, a splinter lodged in the heart of our humanity. Without it, would we have developed so many philosophies, so many metaphysical responses, so many myths? Psychoanalysis, for its part, has definitively declared death to be beyond the reach of the mind, and has turned away from it as a question, abandoning it as fodder for the philosophers and concentrating instead on death in life—which is to say, on mourning.

If death is the cause of such anguish, is it not because it sends us back to the real questions, the ones we evaded, thinking that we would consider them later, when we were older and wiser and had the time to ask ourselves the essential questions?

Those who approach death sometimes discover that the experience of the beyond is already sketched out for them in the very experience of life, here and now. Doesn't life lead us from one beyond to the other, beyond our selves, beyond our certainties, beyond our judgments, our egoism, beyond the world of appearances? Doesn't it invite us to a constant dance of forward movement, followed by a fallback into questioning, then superseded by a forward surge once again?

This book will try to explore a miracle. When death comes so close, and sadness and suffering rule, there is still room for life, and joy, and surges of feeling deeper and more intense than anything known before.

In a world that believes a "good death" to be abrupt—if possible, unconscious, or at least fast, so as to cause the least upset to the survivors—I believe that an act of witness to the preciousness of these last moments of life and to the extraordinary privilege of being able to share them has some value. Better still, I hope to make some contribution to the evolution of our society: toward one that would teach us to integrate death into life, instead of denying it; toward a more humane one, in which we would use an awareness of our own mortality to deepen our respect for the value of life itself.

I HOPE to be able to open up my readers' minds to the rich rewards that come from being there to share the last living moments of someone close to them. I have made my own discovery of these rewards over the years, and it has transformed my life. No matter what we often believe, dying is not an encounter with nothingness, devoid of all meaning. Without detracting from the pain of this journey through mourning and renunciation, I would like to show how the last interval before death can also be the culmination of the shaping of a human being, even as it transforms everyone else involved. There is still time for many things to live themselves out, on a different plane, more interior and more subtle, the plane of human relations.

Even when one enters final helplessness, one can still love and feel loved, and many of the dying, in their last moments, send back a poignant message: Don't pass by life; don't pass by love. The ending of the life of someone you love can allow you to accompany that person to the very last step. How many of us grasp this opportunity? Instead of looking oncoming death squarely in the face, we behave as if it will never come. We lie to one another, we lie to ourselves, and instead of giving voice to the essential, instead of exchanging words of love, or gratitude, or forgiveness, instead of leaning on one another for support in the extraordinary "crossing" that is the death of someone we love, pooling all the wisdom, the humor, and the love of which we're capable for the moment of actual encounter, we allow this final, essential, unique moment of life to be mired in silence and solitude.

This book is the fruit of seven years of accumulated experience in the company of the dying who have come to spend their last days in a palliative care unit in Paris. It is also the fruit of several years of working with people who are HIV-positive, and with AIDS patients hospitalized in a unit for infectious diseases.

It has woven itself from the thread of my own thoughts, and those of people close to me. I would like to thank them all for these conversations.

For reasons of confidentiality, most of the first and last names in the book have been changed. Dr. Clement is an invented character, a composite of various doctors I have met in recent years.

Intimate Death

◇ ◇ ◇ ◇ ◇ ◇ ◇ ◇ ◇ ◇ ◇ ◇ ◇ ◇ ◇ ◇ ◇

I AM at Bernard's bedside. He has just moaned softly, and his hand crept out and squeezed mine. "My angel," he whispered with extraordinary tenderness.

Bernard is dying of AIDS, living out his last days at the palliative care unit where I work. He's a friend, only forty years old. The illness has furrowed his face and emaciated his body, but an enduring youth and symmetrical beauty still show in his features. This beauty, which has preserved itself in all its fragile vulnerability despite everything, moves me.

We have made each other a promise, and now I am here beside him, keeping that patient, emotional vigil that we call "accompanying" someone.

TWO WEEKS ago, I interrupted my vacation for a quick trip to his bedside. He sensed that he would die soon, and this mirrored my own instinct that I should see him as soon as I could. It was an instinct that obviously sprang from the depths of the soul. So I spent

August fifteenth with him. We were utterly gentle with each other, and utterly candid; the day stays with me as part of my private treasure trove of happiest memories.

Now that I really have come back from my vacation, to find him so weak that he almost cannot speak anymore, I am so glad I had an intuition that I must see him again while he could still express himself fully in words. We talked a great deal about his life, about friends we share, and also about his death, which he was now awaiting with a mixture of curiosity and relief. He made me an offering of a treasured old silver bracelet that he'd found in the street in southern Egypt, saying, "It's time for me to give the things I love to the people I love."

THERE is no doubt that the fact of that day together, which really allowed us to say our good-byes, means that I can now sit here beside him, not waiting for any moment in particular, feeling completely at peace, savoring in my heart of hearts this extraordinary gift of his last moments of animate life.

For our sharing of experience is ongoing, although on a different plane. It is hard to find words for this intimate, secret joy; seen strictly from outside, this vigil could seem sad, depressing, uncommunicative, endlessly slow, endlessly long. Everything is so subtle, so fine-drawn. And I feel him so vividly present.

YESTERDAY, for example, we bathed him. An hour's well-being for this numbed body, stiff from lack of

4

movement, all skin and bone. An hour's gentle affection that I shared with Michèle, the nurse, and Simone, the auxiliary.

Very gently, we surrounded this body as it abandoned itself trustingly to the warmth of the water. Three loving women busy with the most sacred task of tending to a dying man. It is a way of taking care of a body that makes one forget all physical damage, because it is the whole person that is being enveloped in tenderness. It is a way of taking care of a dying man that allows him to feel that his soul is alive until the very end.

And that was when Bernard, who seemed so exhausted and already so far gone from us, roused himself as if from a long sleep to plant a tiny soft kiss on the back of my hand. I was so elated! How could this one gesture have had such a galvanizing effect on me? I was suddenly light, happy, full of life. One little kiss on a wet hand, last token of affection from a dying man in his bath.

"You know, friendship is what matters most to me." They are Bernard's first words in twenty-four hours, almost inaudible, struggling to emerge from his exhausted, breathless body. They are also, although I will only realize this later, the last words he will ever utter.

IT'S NIGHTTIME. I've decided to spend it here with Bernard. Everything on the shift is quiet. The chubby little nurse, so young and full of life, has just brought me an herbal tea. She sat down beside me so sweetly—a way of saying, I'm here, I'm keeping you company. Our heads touched for a second, and I felt my tears well up, the kind that heal you and ease your heart. People who spontaneously express compassion probably have no idea how much good they do. Unconsciously, they are encouraging those they touch to allow themselves to yield to the flux of their emotions.

YES, I'M IN PAIN. Why not admit it?

I WATCH Bernard in the pale glow of the night-light. His eyes are wide open, but he doesn't see me. They are staring, huge, almost terrifying in the thinness of his face.

His emaciated chest heaves with the desperate struggle to breathe as my hand tries to soothe the chaos as gently as possible.

The agonizing rasping as the throat congests: What should I do? Summon the nurse, who will insert a probe and aspirate the phlegm that now keeps accumulating in his trachea? Force him to submit to that ultimate aggression, which is nonetheless necessary if he is not to suffocate?

I'VE NEVER been so unhappily aware of my own powerlessness when faced with the necessity of a painful medical intervention. What can I do, other than envelop Bernard in every ounce of my affection while the nurse is working on him? And then massage him, stroking him gently to calm him again. More than once, I put on Schubert's "Ave Maria," and the warm voice of Jessye Norman, which Bernard loves so much, envelops the two of us.

AND SO the night unfolds slowly, broken by these moments of inevitable torture. I know Bernard is ready to die; he's been preparing for it for eighteen months. Why is it such agony?

"BERNARD, I'm remembering when you were hospitalized up on the fifth floor, for your first toxoplasmosis. You were scared stiff. You were sure you were going to die from one day to the next. You were feeling so tormented that you decided to take things into your own hands. Do you remember? You swallowed your signet ring and then a nail, and then you even tried to jump out of the window."

Bernard is looking at me now. He's listening, and he gestures for me to go on. It's as if he wants me to tell him his own story.

"You didn't want to live anymore. You couldn't see your way into any future; you couldn't imagine a slow road to death. And you felt so guilty!

"I talked to you a lot about those nighttime journeys, when you cross a desert in despair because you cannot see any end to it, nor what's up ahead. But I also told you that you would come through those terrible stretches, and that's when you discover strengths you didn't know you had. I remember you said, 'Do you believe that?' I was about to go away for a week and I wanted to give you the strength to believe it before I left. I answered, 'I'm absolutely sure,' with an assurance that astonished me. A week later, when I came back to the hospital, I met your dear Dr. Tirou, and he told me it was a real miracle: Everything was all right again and you were in great shape. I rushed to your room. You were sitting on your bed, with the most wonderful look on your face, and you threw your arms around me. 'I want to live,' you said to me, and I was so moved that all I could say was, 'I want to help you do it.'

"You know, Bernard, you're one of the people I've learned most from. I've watched you live and fight this illness, and I've seen you transform yourself. You showed me that it's possible to face one's own death and go on living and giving meaning to one's life. I remember the day when I broke my arm and you came in a taxi to take me to your osteopath. In the waiting room, in front of two absolutely flabbergasted middle-aged women, you told me what you wanted done with your body. The two women stared incredulously at this forty-year-old man, a bit thin, perhaps, but radiating energy, talking about his own death and where he'd like his ashes to be scattered— in that little corner of Italy that he loved, under the olive trees. I looked at you. You were breathing life that morning, and talking to me about death as if it were quite natural. I thanked you as deeply and personally as I knew how for having let me witness such a thing.

" 'You see, I've sorted everything out now, and I think I'm at peace with everyone. I can go on living or I can die from one minute to the next. I'm ready,' you said to me. That was three months ago. You made such progress in the eighteen months from the day you collapsed into despair because you'd just been told you had AIDS."

I am trying, lovingly, to pull together all the moments of his life that I've shared. It feels like a sacred task: I see myself weaving together two golden threads, his life insofar as I have encountered it, and my life in these last months, overturned by his. For there's no casual rubbing along with anyone who feels the touch of death and recognizes it and is living everything that happens as if it were a gift. From him, I've learned to be grateful for every instant granted.

Now I'm in the act of unrolling our friendship at the feet of this dying man like a bolt of precious cloth. There's so much I wish I could say to him in these moments, about how much he's helped me to change.*

His window, which looks onto the grounds, is beginning to let in the first light of the new day—his last day. Bernard will die at seven o'clock this evening. One friend will have just left him, another will be on her way, arriving a few minutes later. Like so many others, he will seem to have waited until he was alone to take his leave.

9:00 A.M. The palliative care team is gathered in the office for the morning coffee break. There are croissants and chocolate rolls. Dr. Clement brought them. When he leaves home in the morning to go to the hos-

---

*After his death and to honor his memory, Jean-Louis Terrangle and I cofounded the Bernard Dutant AIDS Association, whose purpose is to help anyone who is HIV-positive to find the strength to live as fully as possible within the confines of the illness.

9

pital, he often remembers the nurses. Some of them arrive there as early as seven o'clock in order to be present when the patients wake up. As he passes the bakery on the rue Coquillière, he makes a stop. It's true that when he comes in with his great smile and his arms full of sweet-smelling breads, warmth and well-being spread like a collective breath through the shift.

The team has assembled for one of those frequent gatherings that are an additional bond in its work.

It's been several years since I joined this team, the first such team to volunteer in France to accompany and care for those at the very end of life.

When I made the choice, I had no conception of how proximity to suffering and the death of others would teach me to live differently, with greater awareness and greater intensity. I didn't know that a place dedicated to receiving the dying can be the diametrical opposite of a house of death—that is, a place where life is manifested in all its force. I didn't know that it was the place where I would discover my own humanity, or that I would in some fashion plunge into the very heart of human life.

Attracted by the smell of hot coffee and Dr. Clement's beaming face, Chantal, the night nurse, decides to linger for a few minutes more. Her shift is over, but she wants to share the fruits of her night's work with the others. Night duty is a solitary task, so she rarely misses an opportunity to spend some time with the day team; it makes her feel less alone. In her characteristic rush of words, she's describing her night. Patricia, the young woman who arrived yesterday, used different pretexts to keep ringing for her during the first part of the night.

Chantal could tell that this patient was in torment.

She says she was hesitating about whether to administer a sedative or not, when she was struck by a shining idea. Getting hold of a tray, she covered it with a white napkin and set it with two pretty cups, a little bunch of flowers, and a lighted candle. After filling the cups with a fragrant, steaming herbal tea, she went to Patricia. It was 2:00 a.m. She describes the surprise and happiness on the young woman's face, and the atmosphere of an intimate celebration that she had been able to create.

Creating this atmosphere of warmth and calm around a sick person who is in torment is unquestionably the most beneficial thing one can do for him or her. Chantal has known this for a long time. The doctors have always been astonished to note that so few tranquilizers or anxiety-reducing drugs are given to patients on the nights when she's on duty. She just prefers to give them a massage or tell them a story, or simply let them talk while she sits quietly at their bedside. That's what she did last night, she says, with Patricia.

WE DON'T yet know Patricia. All we've learned is that she has cancer of the uterus, which has now spread, and that she can no longer stand up. Like all the patients we serve, she's in the terminal phase of her illness. Like them, she has spent a long time undergoing all sorts of unpleasant treatments, which she bore courageously because her life was at stake and everything had to be tried in order to cure her. But her illness got worse, and the doctors concluded that there was no more to be done. Was there anything left that could help her? Her oncologist had to tell her husband, Pierre, that he had run out of possible treatments. "How long do you give her to live?" Pierre asked in a strangled voice. The doctor replied that there was no accurate way of predicting how much time remained to any patient "condemned by medical science."

BUT IF there is nothing more to be done, medically speaking, does that mean that the dying person is beyond help? Are they not fully alive until the very last moment? The oncologist advises Pierre to get in touch with this new palliative care unit in Paris. He assures Pierre that she'll be taken care of there until the very end, that they'll make her comfortable and make sure she doesn't suffer, and that they'll help her to live her last moments the way she wants. And Pierre, too, will find the support he needs to accompany his wife in this last ordeal.

DR. CLEMENT, who received the couple when they arrived, tells us that Patricia has not been told of the bad prognosis for her illness. Nor has she been told exactly what a hospice is. The term she's been given is *convalescent home*. In his tactful way, Dr. Clement tried to find out what Pierre thought of this conspiracy of silence surrounding Patricia. From what he can tell, Pierre isn't ready to break it yet; he's afraid that Patricia will collapse, that she'll lose all joie de vivre, and that in taking away all hope, he'll kill her.

It's not the first time we've heard these arguments, which show just how deeply the common view of death is colored by anguish. We think we're protecting the person who's dying, but aren't we first and foremost trying to protect ourselves? What do we know of the innermost feelings of the dying? Do we not underestimate their capacity to face things squarely?

Dr. Clement talked this through with Pierre at length. First of all, he reassured him that nobody here would allow him- or herself to make any presumption about the amount of time left to live. The time remaining to anyone "condemned by medical science" belongs absolutely to him or her. One might say that it's a deep and intimate secret and that the only person in possession of it is the one directly concerned.

However, the fact of being unable to forecast the amount of time remaining is not a license to keep anyone in a state of false hope about a cure. On that point, Dr. Clement is categorical. If Patricia asks him direct questions about how her illness is evolving, he will tell her that he has used up his medical resources and has no means to make her better. It is never easy for a doctor to admit to this powerlessness. Trained to heal, he almost instinctively views death as a defeat. This doctor, consumed by a passion to cure, in love with life, the father of four children, has bravely had to call into question all his own attitudes in order to accept his own limitations, and in so doing, he has added a deeper dimension to his work.

LIKE many of his fellow doctors, Dr. Clement was borne along for many years by the myth of omnipotence. He experienced the golden age of medicine, when extraordinary technological strides were made and death was forced back on one front after another. He acknowledges that he felt himself to be invested with enormous power and responsibility to save human life. Of course, it happened that some of his patients did not get better. They underwent specialized courses of treatment and usually died in the hospital. The doctor never liked this. He felt defeat, sadness, guilt. And then someone close to him died. Sometimes you have to be touched by something personally in order to see things differently—to see, for example, that if illness is an enemy to be fought, death is not. What can one do against it? There are certain moments in life that perhaps make us understand more fully that death is part of life, and that it is inevitable. At these moments, there are two ways of reacting: to face it or to run away. Dr. Clement made his choice. His career led him to take on a hospital job and to live even more closely with death. Instead of concentrating on the machinery of the body in order to preserve life at all costs, he chose to relieve pain, to watch over the comfort of his dying patients, and to accompany them to the very end.

Pierre came away from his conversation with Dr. Clement somewhat comforted. We were going to teach ourselves to listen to Patricia, to respect her silences and also her questions. We would help her move toward greater truth, but only by her own choice.

EVERYONE around the coffee table has listened attentively to Dr. Clement. The nurses are grateful for the chance to discuss their patients like this with a doctor. It hasn't always been the case for them. Most of them come from staffs where each individual remains isolated in her own duties, where they never all gather together to talk about what the patient is going through, far less what this is also doing to the nurse, and the pain involved.

Accessibility is what is probably most lacking in people's relations with one another in the hospital. Here, on this staff, I believe that it is our availability, one to the other, that allows us to support one another and to share this weight of grief.

The coffee bowls are washed, the table wiped off. Everyone gets ready for the morning ahead. Dr. Clement lays an affectionate hand on my shoulder. "Come, Marie, let's go and see Patricia."

"GOOD morning, Patricia! I would like you to meet Marie, our staff psychologist. She will be able to help you if you need her. I think you had a celebration last night?"

As he's talking, the doctor makes himself comfortable on a chair to the left of the bed. Patricia acknowledges me with a big smile. I am struck by her beauty and radiant charm. As she tells the doctor about the ups and downs of the night, I have time to observe her. No sign of the mortal illness that is devouring her shows in her face, with its flowering, generous Eurasian beauty, framed in luxurious long black hair. The fresh orchid she has pinned into it says a great deal about the care she takes of herself, or perhaps about her desire to remain attractive, come what may. I think back to the way Pierre spoke about her to Dr. Clement, as if she were a child-woman to be protected.

"And last night's distress—what was going on inside you?" Dr. Clement has taken her hand, as if to signal her that he's ready to discuss it.

"I keep asking myself, Doctor, it's been a month since I've been able to walk, and I can see it's not getting any better. Please tell me—will I be able to walk again?"

Dr. Clement throws me a glance that I know well, a mixture of courage and distress. He knows he's about to embark on something difficult, and he wants me there as a support. He moves a little closer to Patricia, and as he talks to her, he looks straight into her eyes, and his voice is delicate. He patiently reviews with her the history of her illness. Yes, she knows she has cancer, and she knows that it's metastasized. They've tried chemotherapy, followed by radiation, but all these have been discontinued because they are no longer effective. They're leaving things alone, but the illness is still there. Yes, that's why she can no longer walk—it's her perineum, with its invasive, painful growth. Yes, they've run out of treatments to make things better. They can only ease the pain. Yes, as things are, walking is a thing of the past.

The moment has come; the blade of truth strikes home relentlessly. It has been dispatched with delicacy but also precision, and no fancy flourishes. There is no other way. To fence about the subject, or leave things vague, would only have deepened Patricia's malaise. That is what has been keeping her from sleeping at night, because she senses things she cannot put into words.

She's racked with tears now. Mourning the loss of one's autonomy is one of the most agonizing tortures there is. Dr. Clement is deeply shaken, but he knows that crying is healthy and that Patricia has no shortcut through this pain. I go to her, and she throws herself into my arms like a little girl, sobbing, "I don't want to die."

Clement gets up. It's my turn now. That's one of the strengths of working as a team. As he leaves the room, I hold Patricia in my arms and rock her gently. Gradually, the sobs begin to space themselves and words come between them.

"I want to live. I don't want to die, not now. I don't want God to take me when I'm not ready."

"You'll have the time you need, Patricia. The time you have left to live belongs to you. It's a secret between your soul and God," I say to her.

I can feel she's comforted. Without even realizing it, she has just exchanged her loss of hope of a cure for a little time yet to live. A few moments later, she even spells out that she needs at least two months.

This sort of bargaining is quite common in people who realize that they're going to die but who still have so much energy to live. They set a date when this investment will mature, be it the marriage of a child, the birth of a grandchild, or some celebration. Once that date has been reached, he or she surrenders gently to the arms of death.

AFTER leaving Patricia, but not before assuring her that she can count on me to support her in difficult moments, I feel the need to be alone for a minute or two. The little smoking room next to the family dining room is empty. It is a quiet place that has already seen much grief. Patients' families and the staff take refuge here when they need silence and solitude, when they need to marshal their strength or just cry.

This brief visit with Patricia has shaken me. One never emerges unscathed from these plummeting journeys into the heart of other people's suffering. How could one not be powerfully moved when one is the silent witness to that most solemn moment when a human being glimpses the approach of death? One day it will happen to me, too. How will I react?

Sitting in one of the comfortable armchairs, I steal a moment's solitude and let my thoughts float free. It's my way of recharging myself. Patricia's plea not to die until she's ready makes me think of Xavier, a friend who died of AIDS a few weeks ago. A year before his death, when he was being revived after an acute attack of pneumocystosis, he said to me, "I'm not afraid of dying, but I don't want to die before I'm ready." In the night, he'd dreamed that he was to go to "the new world"—America, no doubt—but that they didn't want to give him his ticket yet. "You'll get it at the right time," he was told. He had asked for time to prepare for death, and life gave him a year. Having seen him frequently during that year, I know that beyond any mere ordering of one's affairs, preparing for death means excavating the bedrock of one's relations with other people, teaching oneself to let go.

People often ask me what drove me to come and work in a place like this, rubbing shoulders with suffering and death. I think two currents have carried me toward it since childhood. The one, more spiritual, sprang from the pain of a death in the family; it's the question without answer that I meditate on every day of my life, and that pushes me forward. The other is my boundless curiosity about the human spirit, which led me to become a psychologist, to explore the field of psychoanalysis and, more recently, that of haptonomy,* the science of affective contact.

LIFE has taught me three things: The first is that I cannot escape my own death or the deaths of the people I love. The second is that no human being can be reduced to what we see, or think we see. Any person is infinitely larger, and deeper, than our narrow judgments can discern. And third: He or she can never be considered to have uttered the final word on anything, is always developing, always has the power of self-fulfillment, and a capacity for self-transformation through all the crises and trials of life.

BORN after the war into a family that had been sorely tested in those years, I grew up in an anxious, over-protective atmosphere. There was never any open discussion of death, but it was in the air all around us, and our lives were subject to all sorts of rituals that were doubtless supposed to protect us from it. Thus I remember that all our walks, when we were on holiday at my grandmother's house, ended at the cemetery. It was a pretty cemetery, surrounded by Beaujolais vines. My grandfather and uncle were buried there. A plaque said that the latter "died for

---

*This concept, created by Frans Veldman, comes from the Greek *hapto*, meaning "to touch, make contact, establish relationship with," and *nomos*, which designates the rules governing physical contact.

France" at the age of twenty-five. We came every day to pray at his grave, carrying heavy watering cans, because there was as yet no running water so far from the village, and my grandmother always wanted the geraniums to be beautiful and in full flower.

This daily visit, which I liked making, since I felt it represented something important, taught me in the most natural way to think about life and death. On my knees, or sitting on the ground, I would look over the little wall that circled the cemetery and gaze at the horizon. The cemetery was on the flank of a hill, and the view stretched endlessly, right over the river Saône and often all the way to the Alps. The days when you could see Mont Blanc were blessed. I would think, and ask myself a thousand questions: Where were this young uncle whom I'd never known and this little child, dead at four, whose grave I was sitting on as I gazed into the distance? What was there after death? A little later, finding no answers, I would get up and start doing things. I had decided to look after a grave that had been left untended since the turn of the century. From what I could tell, nobody had come for a very long time to pray for the young man, a priest, who had also died at the age of twenty-five. The iron fence around the gravestone was rusty and there were never any flowers. I had taken the grave under my protection and had started to repaint the iron, and brought my little bunch of wild flowers every evening to lay on the weathered stone.

It's only now that I realize how much this daily ritual helped prepare me for my work today: lifting the taboo on death and restoring it to its place at the center of our lives.

Far from making me depressed or morbid, this familiarity with death and the meditation on it gave me a passionate taste for life and pleasure, and a voracious curiosity. I drew enormous energy from it.

NONETHELESS, there were times when I experienced terrible bouts of anxiety. I understood later on that I was absorbing like a sponge my parents' own anxiety, their fear of any separation, any break. My precocious anxiety about death was that mine would be the cause of immense pain to others.

And then some years later, my grandmother died, and her last words were, "Oh the light—so it's true!" That's when I knew, in my heart of hearts, that death in and of itself is nothing so very consequential, just a passage into a mysterious dimension. What was absolutely of consequence, however, was the agony of separation, and, for some people, dying without ever having truly and intensely lived.

Life was precious. The idea that one must make something of it, accomplish something, came to me very easily.

AND THEN there was the death of my father. It was a brutal death, unanticipated and cruel. A self-administered death, at the age of eighty-two, done with his pistol—incomprehensible then, incomprehensible now. I will never know why he did it. What I do know all too well, on the other hand, are the weight and the pain of disappearance, when there has been no way to say good-bye. Everything I would have wanted to say to my father and had no time to say to him—words, gestures of love and gratitude

—and my not being there when he was dying— certainly added their weight to my decision some years later to dedicate myself to accompanying others on the last steps of life's journey.

MARIE-HÉLÈNE, a gentle, calm young woman who gracefully performs her duties as supervisor, tells me that a new patient has arrived. In a few words, she draws a heartbreaking picture of the situation: A seventy-year-old woman, mentally confused, with uterine cancer that has metastasized in all directions, is in such a state of agitation and anxiety that they've had to raise the bars on both sides of her bed. And they're worried that she may try to climb over them. So there will have to be someone with her at all times. For the moment, her daughter, who came with her, is at her bedside. She, too, seems to be in a dreadful state.

After taking just enough time to put my bag in my office and pull on my white coat, I'm in the doorway of room 775. I always take a split second to compose myself before walking into the room of a new patient. Each encounter, I know, is a new adventure. But the first encounter with someone who is preparing to die commands particular attention and respect. We are never sure if we shall see this person again.

ON THE BED, I see a shapeless figure, a panting body racked with sudden agitated movements, face drawn, eyes haggard, a wild disorder of long white hair. This woman is a painful sight. Standing on the right is her daughter, in visible consternation at this spectacle, anxiously observing each movement her mother makes. To the left of the bed is Simone, the nurse's aide, calm and smiling, a little flame of reassurance in this vision of hell. Marcelle, our patient, is a former factory worker, brave, self-possessed, who struggled to live and bring up her children. Now she rambles incoherently, interrupted by wild swings of her arms and desperate attempts to clamber over the bars. Her daughter and Simone can barely restrain her.

Just as I arrive at her bedside, a word detaches itself from the flood of babble: *die*. This word, once released, bobs up repeatedly like a stick hurled out of nowhere into a mad torrent. And every time she hears the dreaded word, Marcelle's daughter goes into a panic herself, begging her mother to be quiet: "Don't say that, Mama. Hush. You're here so that they can take care of you and make you better."

As if commenting on this false piece of comfort, Marcelle starts struggling even harder. Simone looks at me. I sense that she wants me to intervene, and I give her a smile of encouragement. Delicately but firmly, she suggests that the daughter leave the room and allow us a few moments alone with her mother.

As soon as the daughter leaves, the mother rolls over toward the nurse's aide, who is bending over her in an attitude of tender attentiveness, which inspires such confidence in the sick. I am witnessing a silent conversation, in which this woman has locked eyes with Simone and seems to be saying, I want to be told the truth. And then, in a clear, firm voice that contradicts everything that has gone before, Marcelle looks at Simone and says, "I'm going to die." And Simone, putting her arms around the patient, replies gently, "We'll be here to accompany you to the very end."

No words of false consolation, no evasion, no fuss. The nurse's aide has merely taken note of what this woman was saying, assuring her by the very attentiveness of her presence that she would not die alone.

Much to our surprise, I must say, Marcelle now sits herself up in bed. Once she is settled comfortably against her pillows, she seems to draw on some inner authority, as if she has recovered her orientation and her senses, then asks for her daughter to be called back into the room. The latter, astonished, as well she might be, by her mother's return to normalcy, approaches nervously.

"I'm going to die," Marcelle says again, in a weak voice, but calmly.

"Mama, you mustn't say that! You should be ashamed of yourself!"

Faced with the emotional disarray of a daughter so clearly unprepared to separate from her mother and the burden that this is placing on someone struggling bravely to meet her own death, I now move closer.

"Your mother is telling us what she feels. We should listen to her and let her tell us what she needs. That's how you can help her best."

Marcelle begins to dictate her last wishes to her daughter, who's standing at her side, weeping quietly. She wants to see all her children, and her grandchildren; she wants to give each of them some last instructions and say good-bye. You can feel that she's herself again, self-possessed, and that it matters to her that she remain so to the very end. It's her particular way of dying with dignity.

Simone and I discreetly leave the room so that our patient and her daughter can organize all the details of what is clearly a farewell ceremony.

"Simone, you were wonderful. You knew exactly what to say, and the effect was almost miraculous!" I say as I give her a hug.

I'm very fond of Simone. With her enormous clear blue eyes and musical voice, this little woman brings so much gaiety and life into our midst. Nonetheless, she has had her own share of suffering, and I know that her life isn't easy, for she's raising her children on her own. Perhaps it's this very quality of spontaneous joie de vivre in someone who understands suffering that moves us so much. One day when I asked her what helped her to be able to take care of people who were so dependent and so physically ravaged, she replied simply, "I tell myself it could be my father or my mother. And so I do for these people just what I'd do for them, or what I'd like someone to do for me if I were in their position."

Suddenly moved, I kiss Simone, who knew how to do such a simple thing to help this woman out of the abyss in which she was struggling, and I suggest we go and have a cup of coffee.

ONCE again, we've just witnessed the fact that the worst kind of solitude when you're dying is not being able to say to the people you love that you're going to die. To feel your death approaching and not to be able to talk about it or to be able to share with others what this leave-taking inspires in you often results directly in mental breakdown, a kind of delirium, or some manifestation of pain that at least gives you something you are allowed to talk about.

As we've seen so often before, the dying person *knows*. All that's needed is some help in being able to articulate that knowledge. Why should it be so hard to say? Isn't it because everyone else's distress makes it hard to talk, and so the dying person has to protect them? Our recent experience with Marcelle confirms that the person who can say to someone else *"I am going to die"* does not become the victim of death but, rather, the protagonist in his or her own dying. It is a moment of standing up straight again, and of the return of an inner strength that nobody else knew was there. The person who can say "I am going to die" can conduct that departure, organize it, as Marcelle is now doing.

Some of the others in the team have joined us for coffee and ask us to replay this scene, and there's also a trainee who's with us from a provincial hospital. In the oncology unit where she works as a nurse, there's a constant feeling of unease around the patients for whom all treatments have failed. The doctors there are no supporters of the "truth." They limit themselves to informing the families, who in turn feel duly condemned to keep everything a secret. The nurses are also subject to the same sentence. Imagine the misery of having to take care of patients who keep looking at you anxiously and keep asking why things aren't getting better. Trapped between the terror of their patients and the cowardice of the doctors, these nurses have no way to share the journey of the dying, and often they go home feeling they have been completely inadequate to the human demands of the situation.

"Here, at least, you never encounter this kind of problem, since the whole team is directed toward candor."

I CAN FEEL the nurse's confusion and her loneliness. Coming in as part of our team, she is learning that the response to this problem of how to communicate with someone who is approaching the end of life is a collective one. What can you achieve on your own? When everyone around you is running away, abandoning the patient? I would like to tell her that despite all this, she really can help her patients.

"If you can just sit for a few minutes and allow your patients to tell you what they're feeling, you will be giving them a lot. If the questions are too pressing—Have I had it? Why are they not doing anything anymore? How much time do I have left?—you can say that you don't know all the answers but that they have the right to ask all these questions. That way, they'll know that you're not afraid, and they'll let you in on what they really feel," I tell her.

THE TEAM is deep in conversation. Someone mentions a sick woman who had been told that the palliative care unit was a "convalescent home." When she arrived, in a state of extreme distress, she kept saying, "I don't understand a thing—they talk about convalescence, but every day I feel weaker," and it didn't take long for her to come out with the straight question to the doctor: "What is going on?" He replied, "*Convalescence* is not the right word. You're in palliative care here, where we can give you every possible comfort and care, and treatment to ease the pain, because your sickness is spreading and we have no means to stop it." Hearing this, instead of collapsing, the young woman let out a sigh of relief. "At least I understand!" She said her distress was rooted in the discrepancy between what she knew deep inside herself—what her body was telling her—and what other people were saying. Now there was harmony between the two. The night that followed this conversation with the doctor, she slept very well. And in the days that followed, she began to prepare for her departure.

"It's true," says one of the nurses, "families always believe that the one who's sick cannot deal with the truth They don't realize that the sick person knows it already, and is carrying that knowledge all alone."

"So how do you help the families?" asks the young trainee.

"I often suggest to people that they try to imagine what would help them if they were the one who was sick. Most people say that they wouldn't want people to tell them stories. Some of them say they would be most concerned about the people closest to them, and that they'd want to reassure themselves about their future."

"And for themselves?" asks a voluntary worker who's come to join the conversation.

"The assurance that they'll be taken care of to the very end, that they'll be helped if they're in physical pain, that they'll be able to hold on to their natural, vital relationships with other people. This last one is what is really denied to patients who are kept in a conspiracy of silence."

IT'S THE END of the afternoon. The team spreads out into the rooms, as it's time to give out medicine and check on the patients' needs. It's also the moment when you can meet the patients' families, who have come to spend the afternoon with them. I encounter Marcelle's daughter, who gives me a big smile. She says she's on her way to phone her brothers and sisters to tell them her mother wants them all to come to her bedside. She is relieved to see that her mother is herself again and that she's taking charge of things. "It's so typical of her," she adds with a catch in her voice. "She taught us how to have the courage to live our lives, and now she's showing us how to die the same way."

BEFORE going off duty, I slip into Patricia's room. It's full of people: her daughter, her husband, friends, and her nine-month-old grandson, who's cuddled up as close as he can, as if to warm her heart. On the table is a vast bowl of exotic fruits. It's a scene full of warmth and life. Patricia's face shows no sign of this morning's distress. I wish her a pleasant evening and a good night and kiss her quite spontaneously, since she invites me to.

ON MY WAY HOME, I can't help but think how enriching even a single day can be. Rich in encounters, rich in contrasts. I'm happy for Marcelle and for Patricia. I know that they both have difficult moments ahead of them, but each of them has demonstrated her own particular kind of inner strength. And I know that this strength will not fail either of them. I also know that my unquenchable confidence is fed daily by all these tiny signs—there for anyone to see—that there is something in us that is larger than we are.

◇

IT IS 9:00 P.M. The place is a good fish restaurant in the Latin Quarter. The man I am having dinner with once asked something of me that was both so important and so intimate that I was dumbstruck.

It happened last summer. We were outside, lying on the grass, enjoying the softness of the breeze on our skin and the heat of the sun on the tiny drops of water still clinging to us after our swim. We were talking about old age and death, and about that time of life we're afraid to enter because we're not sure we can steer through it by ourselves, and because the very idea of being dependent is intolerable. This man, to guard against the extreme threat posed by the loss of his faculties, had decided that when he turned sixty-five he would kill himself. It was, he said, his one and only freedom: to choose the moment of his own death. One thing cast a shadow over him, however, and that was the knowledge that he would have to die in hiding, and alone. Angrily, he spoke of the way Bruno Bettelheim had had to commit suicide, seeing himself reduced to something so archaic as putting his head into a plastic bag and suffocating, just like that, in his lonely corner. Was there no way to recognize humankind's right to die by choice, and for there to be companionship in that end?

There was something close to despair in his voice. I knew that he was in earnest, and I gave him my complete attention. What exactly was he asking? That I perform euthanasia? kill him? I felt something violent inside me—nobody can ask someone else to take life away. Everything in me revolted against the idea. I felt the onrush of circumstantial arguments: Have you thought of other people, of all the people who love you? Why convince yourself in advance that old age is going to be unendurable? There are old people who live out their lives in a glow of light and wisdom—why shouldn't you be one of them?

But what's the point? I thought. He's already heard all that. That's when I decided to listen more deeply to what he was trying to say to me.

"I don't want help committing suicide, nor that anyone should be my accomplice or in agreement with what I'm doing. I just want to know why someone couldn't be there with me as a silent witness, so that I'm not alone. Someone who could stay with me, not able to do anything for me or trying to change my mind, not offering me another way of seeing things, just someone to stop it being said that I died alone."

That was when I caught a glimpse, through the turmoil of feelings and ideas set loose in me by this strange request, of the degree of humanity required of such a passive, powerful witness, and of the barren road that would have to be traveled in order to accompany him in this act that I deemed to be absurd but which was his own, his particular way of dying. I was moved, and I said yes. Yes, if you ask me this, although I disapprove utterly of what you are doing, yes I will be there with you, so that you will not be alone and so that you will know you are loved until the very end.

Now, sitting over grilled sole and chilled white wine, we go back to this pact, sealed on a summer afternoon but still, nonetheless, an imaginary pact, divorced from reality. There's something on my mind that I hadn't wanted to talk about back then, because the important thing was to pay attention to such a request for love. I say how astonished I was by the way he sounded as he defended his right to dispose of his own life. I remind him of the violence and harshness in his voice, as if he were facing some threat to his property, and I remind him of the look in his eyes, cold and blue, as sharp as a blade. Who and what was attacking him? Who was the opponent from whom he must wrestle this ultimate freedom? The question hangs there, and I can feel him acknowledge it. As for myself, I am no longer sure if I can hold to such a commitment. He knows this. That's what we're talking about now. It seems to me, on the one hand, that I could just be there passively so that he wouldn't be alone, but, on the other hand, this strikes me as absolutely unthinkable. I don't know anymore—I'm unable to think, as can happen when one is caught at the heart of a contradiction. He's listening to me. To my great surprise, he tells me that the problem has gone away. Just because I paid attention to his request and took it seriously. Now he's talking to me from the depths of himself, from quite a different place. His voice is steady, calm, and warm, and his eyes are full of tenderness. He has a new way to view the approach of his sixty-fifth birthday. Now there's room for other perspectives, open ground. The last months have witnessed the natural unfolding in him of this openness to new possibilities for his old age. It has been accompanied by a new openheartedness that enlarges the present and thus the future. Perhaps he also has more confidence in what life still holds for him.

I LISTEN to him, and I'm happy. Not because he seems to be abandoning his idea of suicide. I'm happy the way one is when a risk has been taken and a danger overcome, the way one can be when doors open onto new landscapes.

ROOM 780. Dominique keeps begging for death. She has been here for three weeks already. At the beginning, she was always up and about in the corridor in a state of near euphoria. The treatment for her pain had worked miracles—she no longer felt any. The nurses were taken with sympathy for this little thin woman, who was retired from the state education system and who chain-smoked and was forthright and spoke freely about her illness and what she knew to be her imminent death. One's favorite kind of patient: lucid, candid, with flashes of humor. Some even went to smoke a cigarette with her in her room as a way of relaxing. There are patients who, without being aware of it, also take care of the people who take care of them. Dominique was one of these, until the day when she took a turn for the worse. For several days now, she has no longer gotten out of bed, and the pain has returned. The doctors were quick to notice that this eased as soon as someone went to sit with her or gave her an extended massage. But it's become hard for the nurses to spend time with her. Dominique keeps saying she wants to die. In the face of such a demand, what can one say or do?

"Do something, I beg you, I can't just stay like this, pinned in bed and waiting to die. I can't bear it!"

Dr. Clement can't bear it, either, and she is beginning to get on the nurses' nerves, as well. A sort of vicious circle is being set up: The patient is demanding something that nobody has the power to grant. The more she demands the impossible, the more she senses the risk of rejection, the more she fears being abandoned and so the more she demands the death nobody can grant her. The doctor's admissions of helplessness—"It's not within my power to decide when you will die"—and his attempts to make her let go—"Just take it easy, Dominique"—are useless.

"Marie, you should go and see her," he tells me.

So here I am, sitting on her bed, looking at the willful face of this woman who wants to die.

"What's everyone waiting for?" she says aggressively. "For me to be reduced to a rag?"

"What do you want us to do, Dominique? To give you death? You know as well as I do that we have no power to do any such thing, even if we have the technical means."

"So you're just going to leave me like this?" she groans. "It's more than I can bear. All this endless waiting. How long is it going to go on?"

Dominique clenches her fists and cries out in what might be mistaken for pain but is actually an expression of suppressed revolt that can vent itself only in a long moan of pain. Hearing this piercing cry, a nurse is already at the door. I signal her that I'm already here. I feel that Dominique needs to release her anger without her cries resulting in any medical intervention—an increase in the morphine dose or giving her tranquilizers. As always, when anger is given a means of expression, relief follows. Dominique is calmer now, almost passive. I move closer, reach out a hand, which she takes and holds in her own.

"I want to die," she says. "Look what I've become."

She tells me about the steps of her calvary, her double mastectomy, the loss of her identity as a woman. She has no further interest in life. The picture is very black, very despairing. I listen with absolute attention. I am there for her, quite simply. Whenever the emotion intensifies, Dominique squeezes my hand. I do the same; our hands have their own conversation. There's a long pause. Then she smiles and says, "You do me good."

"Are you sure?" I ask. "That you have finished living?"

She seems surprised by my question. "Finished living?" I sense that she's deep in thought, perplexed. "What do you mean by that?" she asks finally.

"Is there anything or anyone tethering you to life, keeping you here?"

I can feel that she's getting more and more intrigued.

"There's no one to keep me here anymore, no, but there are so many things still unsettled," she says wearily.

There, I feel the fish bite the hook. So there's something unfinished in the air.

"Do you want to tell me about it? It might help."

As I have time for her and she can feel it, she sits up and lights a cigarette. For the next hour, she tells me the story of her life, carries me along in her wake through eddies of disappointed love, betrayals, attempts to preserve her integrity in the midst of what she considers the general mediocrity of the public bureaucracy. She confides her innermost pain at having been unable to help her life's companion from sliding into insanity. A touching life, which she reassembles piece by piece in front of me, with, underneath it all, a simple concern: to find the thread that binds each fragment together and gives it all sense. I tell her how much I respect the life she's lived. Her face lights up—she's found it.

"So this is all me," she says. "This is my life."

"It's your life," I say, with the emphasis on *your.*

The silence that follows holds neither lament nor discomfort. Dominique has fallen asleep, and on her face there's a tiny smile of triumph.

IN THE NEXT room, there's a dying man who also demanded loud and long three months ago that his life be ended. As soon as he arrived in the unit, he insisted authoritatively that he "be given the injection."

"I know exactly where I've gotten to. I know I'm going to be that much worse every day. I see no reason to wait for the inevitable!"

Dr. Clement simply said, "You're not dying right now. We'll talk about this again later."

THIS man, a former fighter pilot, loved to recount his exploits and all those intense moments when he had put his life at risk. In the days that followed, we watched him detain this or that nurse or voluntary worker from the team at his bedside. He loved company and took obvious pleasure in exercising his seductive powers as a raconteur. Not one of the personnel or the nursing team believed that this man had done with life. But despite all this, every day he reiterated to the doctor that he wanted euthanasia.

One day when I happened to be with him, he surprised himself by starting to tell me about a time in his life that he had thought he'd written off. It had to do with his first marriage, and the two daughters from that marriage. Not a happy story, and one he didn't care to remember. So why on earth was he coming back to it now? His daughters must be around thirty now, but he had lost all touch with them. Why was he feeling this weight on his heart? I risked the question. "Wouldn't you like to see them just once more?"

"Well, maybe," he said.

From that day on, there was no more talk of euthanasia. The unit secretary's patient researches finally paid off. His daughters were located. They hurried to get to him, and after an extraordinarily touching reunion, they took turns at their father's bedside to accompany him on his final journey. One of them is a nun, the other a nurse, and theirs is the gentle, calm presence in which he is now moving toward death.

❖

THE COMMON room fills up with the various members of the team as they arrive one by one. It's noon, when everyone comes together daily to touch base on the patients, on what course to follow or on what attitude to adopt in this or that situation. Today, the main topic is all these requests for euthanasia from incoming patients, or, indeed, from others at a later point, such as Dominique. What are these requests concealing? We're sure they're a way of articulating the intolerable in this situation. Is it possible to decode something so impossible in the living of it? Is there any way to respond that is better than superficial? There's definitely an attempt at communication here. What are they trying to tell us?

I raise the case of our fighter pilot, Jacques, commenting on how far things have come since his first requests for an injection. Was this man not trying to establish some sense of how long he still had to live? By agreeing to his wishes, would we not have robbed him of his death? The reunion with his daughters would not have taken place, and instead of ending his life in peace, surrounded and cradled in the affection of his children, he would surely have died in turmoil and misery.

And Dominique? I tell the team my impression that her cries of pain and complaint are the cover for deep anger, not just against life but against herself, and that putting words to her anger allowed it to subside. I say that she told me many things still needed to be settled, and that her desire to put an end to it all was part and parcel of all this.

"Last night, everything was peaceful, and when I was taking care of her this morning, there was no talk about wanting to die," one of the nurses says. "Dominique was even pleasant, and called us 'dear.'"

Dr. Clement heaves a sigh of relief. Then, going back to his folders, he says worriedly that two more patients in the unit have asked for their lives to be terminated. "Paul, a young man with AIDS, and Marie-France, a lady of seventy who has facial cancer. We'll have to be on the lookout," he winds up.

Has even he not learned here that the main thing is never to prejudge?

◇

OUR PILOT died during the night. When I come on duty, I start by going to spend a few moments by his body. The usual hospital rules are relaxed here, and the bodies of our patients can remain in the rooms for six hours. This gives the families time to gather in the place where so many words have been said, so many kisses exchanged, last gestures of love that will engrave themselves forever. The nurses and the aides take particular care in washing and arranging the body in bed. There is nothing artificial in their efforts to make the person they have been tending with all possible attention and respect look as good as possible.

This rite of laying out the corpse is their opportunity to pay tribute one last time. It is no surprise to discover all sorts of little attentions! This or that perfume, a particular dress, a flower in the hair or tucked into the hands folded on the sheet bear witness to their desire to honor the dead. Under the touch of their loving hands, faces seem to find peace, seem to relax, and sometimes suddenly look stunningly young again. To the next of kin, these last caring gestures by the nurses are like a balm: It is such a comfort to be able to have a last memory of a face that has passed through suffering and reached peace again.

Dear Jacques is lying there in his old uniform, looking younger, and serene. His beautiful sharp profile seems strangely to have softened itself. There's a hint of a smile on his lips, as if he's asking us not to be sad. His daughters are at his side, praying. They indicate with delicate gestures that I should join them. They have lit a candle and a stick of incense, and this little hospital room gives off an atmosphere of meditation like the one that greets you at the door of an old Romanesque chapel.

❖

FILLED WITH that particular sense of peace that comes over me each time I meditate by the side of someone who has just died, I turn toward Dominique's room. She looks as if she's asleep, but one eye opens as she senses my arrival, and I am greeted with a huge smile.

"Things have been going on inside me since our conversation yesterday. Of course I haven't said all my good-byes, since all my closets are still full of old skeletons," she starts a little hoarsely. "In particular, a sister I haven't seen for three decades. And I don't want to see her again now; I'd just like to be able to tell her I forgive her."

We both try to work out some way to settle this last concern of hers. Dominique finally opts for a letter, which I offer to write down if she dictates it to me. Searching for the best words, she fine-tunes her letter, which she wants to be both serious and modest.

"Dear Léa, my life is almost over. Before I go, I would like you to know that I no longer bear you any grudge. I am going in peace, and I hope you are at peace, too. Please do not try to see me. Things are as they should be."

◇

PATRICIA'S door stands open. Seeing me in the corridor, she motions for me to come in. Less than an hour ago, I was in something that felt like a chapel, and now I'm in the Seychelles next door. The room is covered with photographs of the islands. Tables and chairs sway under their burden of exotic flowers and baskets of fruit. Patricia is more radiantly beautiful than ever, and yet there's a shadow of distress deep in her eyes. We know she knows that this is no convalescent's bedroom, and even if it matters that the room be gay and full of life, she cannot forget that the illness is eating away at her beautiful woman's body. Now she's huddled in my arms, because she is completely simple and spontaneous in the way she makes contact with other people and comes in search of all the tenderness she needs so much. We stay like this for some time. Then she lets go in the natural way a child does after a cuddle. Now she's hunting in the drawer of her night table for a cassette of religious chants she wants me to listen to. It's what she puts on, she tells me, when she's very down. It calms her. In fact, as I discover, she doesn't just listen to these chants; she sings along in a rather pretty voice.

Coming out of her room, I meet Pierre, her husband. "You were right," he says. "I thought she was too much of a child to deal with the truth, but I find she's strong. Now she's rebuilding *my* morale, can you believe it?" His eyes are full of tears, which he brushes away clumsily before going in, his back a little hunched from all the weight he's been carrying these last months.

◆

THE HOSPITAL of Our Lady of Good Help has just opened a little unit of ten beds, the AIDS unit, designated to receive and take care of people who are HIV-positive. A beautiful, dynamic woman has been put in charge. Particularly sensitive to the exclusion of the most disadvantaged, Tristane has always tried to practice medicine humanely and has sworn to help humanize the hospital. So when her chief gave her these ten beds, she organized the project so that it could serve as a general example. With a voluntary, highly motivated team of nurses and aides, she used an existing formula to set up the major guidelines for the unit: the linking of technical and human skills, caring for the person before caring for the symptom, and accompanying patients to the very end, respecting their dignity. The first patients to be admitted very quickly understood the spirit behind this little hospital unit, in which the nurses call them by their first names, in which the doctors take the time to sit at their bedsides and explain the treatments and procedures, and also to listen to their questions, their doubts, and their despair. A unit where they're not just a number among other numbers, where they're quite simply somebody. A unit with an awareness that each room holds an entire human life imprisoned within it, not just a sick body. Most hospitals underestimate this aspect, which is so crucial for anyone who may spend years in and out of such a unit.

After some months, feeling the need to bolster the team with a psychologist who can listen to both the patients and the staff, Tristane, who has been a friend for years, asks me to come and join her. She knew of my experience in a palliative care unit and wanted her team to take on this same task of accompanying people.

Which is how I now come to be here three times a week.

In a little ground-floor room that looks out onto some tall trees, Patrick is waiting for me. He's young, as are almost all our AIDS patients. His friend died two years ago of the same thing. Now it's his turn to wait. He arrived a few weeks ago in pitiable condition, emaciated, weak, with KS (Kaposi's sarcoma) lesions all over both legs. It's been a year since he accepted any kind of treatment, shutting himself in his apartment instead, completely closed in on himself.

"It's as if I'd abandoned myself," he said when talking about this period. "I watched myself letting my body go, as if it were happening to someone else. It felt as if there were two of me. These legs I could see weren't my legs. I looked at the Kaposi and I didn't feel a thing."

Since Patrick is a very solitary person, his family did not become worried by this silence. There had already been long intervals during which he gave no sign of life. "One day, I decided to go to a hotel in Brittany. I took a room with a view of the sea. There I was suddenly afraid: I felt cut off from the whole world. I called my family and I told them I was HIV-positive. I cannot utter the name of my illness. It's

43

just a word, but it's a word that terrifies me, because it's death. I just can't say it."

NOW HE FEELS more connected to reality, and the nurses are taking care of his legs. Changing the dressings is extremely painful, but he allows himself to be taken care of. He no longer has the feeling of total alienation. Curiously, the fact that his body is being tended liberates his spirit. He thinks a great deal about his future—what will it be?—and about his family, which he sees in a completely new way, and whose love and solidarity he is discovering, to his own astonishment.

It's not that these things weren't there before, but that he himself wasn't there to receive them, barricading himself against all contact, protecting his intimacy and his choices in life and in love. One benefit of his illness is that he is discovering the pleasure of being looked after. As he's doing better from every point of view, there's talk of letting him go home to be nursed there.

"Good morning, Patrick. So I hear you're going home soon!"

I sit on the edge of the bed and Patrick takes my hand in his. I look at his finely chiseled face with its regular features and his eyes, whose frankness has touched me since we first met. Patrick is exceptionally handsome. I can imagine the role this beauty must have played in his life. He says that he has always been very sensitive to beauty in both people and objects. It led him to art. He creates contemporary jewelry, which he designs himself, and his greatest pleasure was always to go to exhibitions. It is completely understandable how intolerable the image of his own slow disintegration has been to him. I take the measure of just how much he must surmount from now on—the horrible encrustations that are gradually invading his legs and make him disgusted with his own body—in order to retain a sense that there is a future for him.

"You know, as soon as I go home, I'm going to start making jewelry again. I've had the incredible luck to have been approached by a wonderful couple who want to go into partnership with me. I will design the jewelry and they will be responsible for getting it made and sold. It feels as if a whole new life is opening up in front of me."

It's impossible not to be shaken by so much moral courage.

A nurse has slipped in discreetly, bringing her cart with its gauze and cotton wool. It's time for Patrick's tumor-filled legs to have their dressings changed. He begs me to stay with him.

"That way, you see, I don't think about my legs. It's horrible to see them; it makes them hurt even more."

"Of course I'll stay," I say, and move closer to him.

Spontaneously, he comes into my arms, and I rock him gently. For her part, the nurse removes the bandages and soiled compresses as gently as possible. I see his legs, which have swelled to twice their size and are almost completely covered with purple or black pustules, which in places have merged into a sort of thick crust. The tumor is growing daily and will soon reach his genitals. My heart clenches at the sight of so much suffering, and I gently cradle young, beautiful Patrick against my body as I would a hurt child.

"If I could be cuddled like this every time they change the dressings, that would be my dream. You're so gentle, and you smell good, and I forget everything else."

That's when I realize Patrick's legs give off an acrid smell that's almost putrefaction. The nurse proceeds unhurriedly, with scrupulous care, to change all the compresses. She doesn't appear to be put off by the smell, or by the horror of this rotting flesh. She goes on with her task, with calm concentration, with a comforting word now and then.

"You're so quiet today, it's a pleasure to look after you."

She's speaking sincerely, because, like all her colleagues, she has learned to overcome a certain queasiness at the sight of blood or wounds or various forms of mutilation, but this is not indifference. In her case, I can feel that she's moved by the wish to do her job well and that she works with a good heart. She's not looking after a pair of legs; she's looking after a whole person. In this case, it's Patrick, whom she's gotten to know a little, and whom she thinks of somehow even outside the hospital. He's the same age as she is, and she watches him evolve with a mixture of curiosity and tenderness. The other day, in one of our team meetings, she was commenting on how much she was changing as a result of her contact with this patient.

THE NEW DRESSINGS have been put on. Patrick is in a state of relief, because after all the pain of the nursing, there's always a wonderful feeling of well-being. The nurse and I settle him comfortably in bed, with a framework of hoops over his legs so that the bed-clothes don't press on him. She opens the window for a few moments, then lights a stick of incense, a pretty way of banishing the last unpleasant smells.

"Tomorrow," she reminds him, "the physio is going to come and make you walk a bit. You have to learn to move with your crutches."

Before leaving, she gives him a big kiss on the cheek. It's this kind of emotional rapport that the staff know how to establish with their patients, and it gives a little unit like this one its human dimension.

NOW IT'S MY TURN to leave Patrick. Promising to go and see him once he's home, I return to the university hospital for the fortnightly meeting I hold with the staff to discuss how we meet the emotional needs of the patients.

I began this kind of regular meeting with the unit after I had undergone additional training in hapton-omy (emotional and physical contact), which has un-questionable effectiveness in opening up avenues of communication in a more human way. Under the guidance of Frans Veldman, one develops and tries to ripen one's human faculties of contact; one learns to "dare" to encounter another human being by touch. It may seem foolish to undergo formal training in order to develop a basic human faculty. Unfortunately, the world in which we all grew up and continue to de-velop is one that doesn't encourage spontaneous emo-tional contact. Certainly we touch other people, but that's when the intention is erotic. Other times, the context is impersonalizing, as in the medical sphere, when one is most often manipulating "bodily objects." What is forgotten is what the whole person may feel.

So there is every reason to sensitize medical people to that particular dimension of human encounter that involves touch and to help them become aware of what is at stake every time they touch someone or someone touches them. Does one treat a foot, a leg, a lung, a breast as if it were a discrete object, the object of medical attention and medical interest, or does one treat a human being who is suffering in a particular part of his or her body and whose whole way of being articulates the way this suffering is being experienced?

We don't spend enough time drawing the attention of healers to the body language of patients, their physical gestures, so we don't help them to be more present when they're taking care of people. Yet we know just how much the quality of someone's presence and the fine focus of their attention can transform the way in which any medical treatment or intervention, even the most aggressive, is perceived by the patients. A Benedictine monk from Solesmes wrote to me recently about his illness, saying how much he had been sensitive to the way the nurses touched him. He could recognize each one of them just by their touch; some of them left him feeling whole when they had been tending to him, and some of them left him feeling in tatters!

In a palliative care unit, the sense of contact is integral to the value of the treatment. It is therefore not surprising that several others on the team have followed me and taken the training, too. It was in order to ensure some kind of follow-up and a way of sharing with the others that I suggested this bimonthly meeting.

THIS AFTERNOON, the staff want to explore how to transform aggressive interventions into loving ones. Even though these interventions are kept to a minimum in any palliative care unit—because the aim is to enhance the quality of whatever time is left to live, rather than to extend its duration—it is still true that some actions are inevitable. Beyond the immediate discomfort, they will clearly give real comfort and relief to the patient. They would include such things as giving exercise to bedridden or paralyzed patients, inserting nasal or urinary probes, aspirating the blocked throats of patients who no longer have the strength to spit, or giving rectal stimulation to constipated patients. In a nutshell, any of these procedures is sheer torture for the staff who have to perform them on weak and dying patients, whose only remaining desire is for peace. It's easy to see why they would want to find the most humane and respectful way to do these things.

THE FIRST THING I do when I arrive is to tell the team about the time I just spent with Patrick. The procedure in question is particularly painful and invasive. Patrick instinctively sought the contact and safety of my arms, and for my part, I made myself available to him, but I was also there for the nurse who had to perform such an arduous task. This hospital room was filled with profound calm, instead of all the tensions that usually occur when two fears converge—the patient's fear of pain and the staff's fear of causing pain. Can the team be organized so that two people always come when it's a question of a procedure that may be painful? One simply to offer her presence, her warmth and attention, while the other, just as attentively, does what has to be done with all possible competence. When three people get together like this, each wishing to draw on the presence of the other two in order to face a difficult moment, a composite being with truly miraculous powers is brought into existence. The nurses' aides who are at the meeting confirm this idea—wherever they go in pairs to give whatever bodily assistance is required by someone who can no longer even move in bed, they are aware of how much the fact of being there for each other and of bringing the patient into this link creates a completely different kind of contact. The movements they so gently make to lift a leg and ease a patient over onto his side synchronize themselves of one accord and flow together without jolts or bumping. When one cleans a bedsore, the other embraces the enfeebled body and just stays there doing nothing but rocking it gently, as I had just done with Patrick.

Now each of the team takes turns lying down on the bed in the empty room we're using for the meeting. It's an exercise for everyone to experience for themselves how *good* it feels to receive a touch that comes without any burden of desire or demand. What does it feel like to lie on your side and be able to rest your head on a welcoming shoulder—when the other person is happy just to be there as a silent presence?

Even if none of the staff is ill, each of them easily grasps the sense of well-being and safety that comes from such contact.

IT'S UNDERSTANDABLE that after a meeting like this, with the exchanges it allows and the new awareness it fosters, the staff are no longer able to encounter the patients in the old way. This is how procedures that are usually experienced as painful or humiliating are infused here with tenderness and respect—the opportunity for a communion.

❖

THIS MORNING, I met Dr. Clement. He would like me to visit the two patients who are each asking that they be given the right to die. He has already assured them that he would under no circumstances impose any aggressive course of treatment, and that the only ones he is giving them are for the prevention of suffering. Yet the demands persist, and he thinks they must be some expression of another order of suffering, psychological or affective. He's counting on me to help him work out what's going on.

MARIE-FRANCE is sitting alone in the armchair next to her bed. I come in and settle myself on the footstool that serves as a low second seat. As I enter, I introduce myself to this woman who has half of her face covered by a major dressing. She turns her head away a little as I do so, betraying her fear of any stranger seeing her for the first time.

"It's nice of you to visit a monster like me. I've come to spend my last days here. All I want now is to die, as quickly as possible."

"I've come to meet you. I'm glad to see you are still able to communicate so well. We'll be able to talk together."

I can feel she's touched by being made aware of her own continuing capacity to tell me about herself. I have confirmed that her inmost identity is intact, even if her face is no longer recognizable as human.

"Oh, I'm not that interesting anymore," she goes on, her voice weary.

"Allow me to disagree. In any case, if you agree, I'll come and talk to you. I already have the sense that you've lived an interesting life, which makes it interesting for me, too. You see we don't treat bodies here; we look after individual people who each have a whole history, and we like to know each person in our care."

"As soon as I arrived, I noticed that, and it was nice not just to feel like a number among a lot of other numbers. But you see, even if I'm made to feel welcome here, I still want to die as soon as possible," she says, watching for my reaction.

"I can understand that."

"But the doctor doesn't want to listen. He says everyone has to wait for death to come in its own good time. But I'm not going to have years of that."

"Do you really believe," I say, taking her hands and looking at her for the first time straight in her one good eye, which is full of bright intelligence, "do you really believe it can last for years? Haven't you yourself observed how fast your illness is advancing?

Why would you still be alive if you really believe your life is over?"

MARIE-FRANCE squeezes my hands very tightly, and in the silence of this shared emotion, we form our bond. Having been through it with them so often, I know that patients need to express their longing for death and to have someone with whom to share the emotion they feel when this desire is acknowledged. But let there be no mistake: Acknowledging someone's genuine desire for death in no way implies that one is agreeing to carry it out. Doubtless it's because doctors are afraid that any acknowledgment will engage them in an impermissible act that they go so far as to reject the very idea that a human being could wish for death. With Marie-France, as is often the case, what she's asking is to be able to state what she longs for, and to be heard. But being heard does not mean being obeyed.

Now that she's been allowed to express her exhaustion with life, she seems calmer. As I leave, I ask if I can come back and see her soon, and she accepts at once.

On my way home from the hospital tonight, I think about all these men and women I meet every day, so wounded in their physical integrity. I think of Patrick. I think of Marie-France and of so many others who have struggled to live and make an existence despite their mutilations. These physical changes often turn them into strangers in the eyes of people who no longer can find any of the familiar reference points, and who therefore find it easier to run away. The same questions come up again and again: "How far will all this go?" "Could anyone still love me?" I think about the responsibility we bear as witnesses to this physical decay. With one look, one gesture, we have the power to confirm someone in his or her sense of indestructible identity, or to reinforce the idea that he or she is nothing more than an object, and a rather distasteful one, a leftover to be discarded if possible.

"It is someone else's gaze that brings me into being," said Lacan. This has never been more true than for those who have to undergo the loss of their self-image. Having seen it happen, I can state that people can finally forget their damaged bodies because they are themselves, because the people around them still look at them with loving tenderness and do nothing to call attention to their physical collapse.

NOT LONG ago, a friend who runs an association that fights AIDS told me the following: His companion was in the last stages of the disease, dying in a slow physical deterioration that is hard to imagine. Each time he visited him, he was driven to find one detail, one physical feature of this person he loved, that he could contemplate with gratitude, even joy, the way he had done before the ravages of illness set in. One day, it was the fine curved profile of his nose; another day, it was the elegant line of his eyelids, or the glowing depth of color in his irises. Following the principle of the hologram, he was evidently trying to experience even the minutest part of his lover's body as the locus of the totality and integrity of this man's salient quality; his beauty. This affirmation has often helped me, too, I admit, when I have found myself at the bedside of people whose bodies have been ravaged by illness. Something of beauty always does survive, even if it is only the color of the eyes.

◇

BEFORE I get back to my apartment, I have a date to meet Louis at the Promenade de Venus. This weekly ritual in one of the brasseries at Les Halles is one that means a great deal to both of us. Louis is a man of around forty, and a very close friend. Stricken by AIDS several years ago, he is conducting a determined fight for survival, though under no illusions about the inevitability of his death, and conscious that his weakened immune system puts him at the mercy of the first passing virus. Knowing my very Jungian passion for dreams, which, far from being the reservoir of our repressed emotions, tell us about the profound wisdom inherent in all humankind, he has made it a habit to come and tell me his. It's another way of attuning oneself to one's emotional depths, and of inviting someone else to come and listen to what is going on.

WE'VE decided to meet in this bistro ever since a lung infection severely curtailed his respiratory functions. Climbing the four flights of stairs of my apartment building to visit me had become a trial. Louis comes in a taxi, and he usually arrives early. Settled on the dark red velvet banquette in one of the dining alcoves, he waits for me, his frail silhouette a little bent, always elegantly dressed, even on the days when he's exhausted. It's still clear that he was once extraordinarily good-looking, even if his emaciation and general bearing—his slow gestures, his shaky walk—now suggest a kind of premature old age. At a distance, I am struck as always by the bright life in his eyes and the utter dignity in his bearing.

"Marie dear, I'm so pleased to see you."

Sitting down opposite him, I take his hands in mine and hold them for a long moment, in acknowledgment of the strength of the bond between us.

And I listen to him.

LOUIS always starts by telling me a dream. Of late, many of them have had to do with death. I am the only person, he says, with whom he can talk about this. His circle of friends, who are immensely positive and supportive, keeps his spirits up constantly. It is quite out of the question that he should try to bring up his fears about death: He feels that nobody could tolerate it. Last time we saw each other, Louis was able to talk about these fears.

"I know all this is going to end quite soon, and there are two things I can't get away from; the fear that I'm going to have to go through uncontrollable physical pain as I'm dying, and the worry that I'm leaving my Lila behind me. Knowing that I won't be there any longer to help her and take care of her after my death, if she should fall ill in her turn breaks my heart."

Louis's pain at the thought of leaving his young wife suddenly reminds me of Saltiel in Albert Cohen's *The Brave:* "This wave of love and tears is because I've realised that I will not be there to help her in her old age one day, I won't be there to help her walk or take her arm so that she doesn't fall, be there to be her support, one last forbidden happiness. What will she do without me then? Who will protect her?"

Louis's distress moves me deeply. Without pretending that I can alleviate it, I still want to reassure him about two things.

"I can arrange to help you. As concerns the pain, I know enough about palliative care to be able to promise you that if you are suffering, we will do whatever is necessary. You know that these days, well-administered antipain treatments reduce it in ninety-five percent of cases. As for Lila, you know how surrounded she is by both family and friends. And you shouldn't underestimate her own inner strength. In any case, you can rely on me. I'll do everything I can to help her."

Louis seems so relieved to have been able to put words to his fears that I'm very moved.

"Now what I've got left is to live the time God grants me, with trust in Him. I could have already been dead a year ago, I know that. I'm only alive because of His grace."

Louis seems quite revived today, even filled with new energy. Confirming my impression, he says he's feeling really good.

"You have no idea how helpful our last conversation was! It's one less thing to carry around. And I feel full of energy. I've decided to start writing a novel—it's an old project of mine. It's time for me to settle down and do it. But above all," he says, pulling out of his Tyrolean jacket a piece of paper on which he's scribbled down last night's dream, "here's my nighttime production! I'm in a Fellini film, *And the Ship Sails On*. I'm one of the characters in the film and I'm looking at my legs. To my great astonishment, I see two pairs of legs, one of which looks like my legs as they are now, all skinny. These legs seem to be in the process of disintegrating, but the other pair is all young, with fine soft skin, like newborn legs. Strange dream!"

As always, I ask Louis to tell me what thoughts he has about the dream. The first thing is that he's amazed to find himself a character in a Fellini film, but he admits with good humor that the film is well chosen: *And the Ship Sails On* is surely a metaphor for death. I confirm that leaving in a ship is one of the recurring symbols in the dreams of people who don't have long to live. So this dream is telling him about his death. But what comes next is absolutely intriguing: two pairs of legs!

"Now here I really get stuck. Am I growing a second pair of legs, the way angels grow wings?" he adds with a chuckle.

"You don't know how right you are, dear Louis. Do you know what this part of your dream makes me think of? That phrase of the apostle Paul: 'But though our outward man perish, yet the inward man is renewed day by day' " (2 Corinthians 4:16).

Louis is silent for a long time at this thought-provoking saying, which contains so much hope.

"I must give you Maurice Zundel's essay on the experience of death," I say. "There's a remarkable passage in it where Zundel goes a very long way. He says that nothing proves that our bodies, if we are truly imbued with humanity, cannot subsist in some way that is, in any case, impossible to imagine, not living in dependence on this world, but in complete liberation from it. Fundamentally, he's referring to a sort of transformation of our biological bodies into their essence or nimbus. But he tells us that this body has to be created in our lifetimes. He talks about the human improvement that has to be achieved: Instead of living like 'cosmic scum' floating on the world of chemistry and physics, we have to become the subjects of ourselves, body and soul. It's absolutely fascinating. I'll bring it for you next time."

"There are moments when I feel so free, you know," Louis says. "Even when my body is limiting me in every direction. I think I've never dared to be so much myself. I say whatever I think with an inner freedom that I never knew before."

Louis describes his life as being separate from him, and rich of its own accord. Since he has recently stopped worrying about his tomorrows, what matters to him most is to savor each and every instant, and be grateful for them. I've always thought that true freedom was this interior acquiescence in the unfolding of things, but hearing Louis say it to me like this has a deep effect on me.

WE SOON say good-bye, but not without looking forward to our next meeting in a few days' time for our "prayer evening." For several years now, a group of friends has come together every two weeks to pray and sing together. It began as an evening of shared friendship, but on these particular nights, it organizes itself around a communal prayer. We felt it important in a world that has lost so much of its spirituality to reintroduce this ritual of collective prayer: a handful of human beings, brought together in the name of what gave birth to them, the ultimate reality, present in each one, here and now. It's a way of making a circle around those who are suffering, as we summon their names into the depths of our thoughts. For several months now, Louis and his wife and then, little by little, other sick people or simply those in search of some spiritual sustenance have joined us.

❖

THIS morning, I pass Helen, a self-effacingly discreet nurse. She tells me that Dominique had had a visit from her sister—so the latter did not respect the wish contained in the note: "Please do not try to see me." At bottom, I'm not surprised. Léa was waiting for some such signal to have a reconciliation with her sister. She must have rushed to the hospital as soon as the letter came.

"Do you know if the meeting went well?" I ask.

"No, all I know is that she spent all night talking to a voluntary worker, and that this morning she's very weak."

The blinds are down in her room, which means that Dominique is still asleep. This is one of those small details that make this unit particularly humane: Nobody wakes the patients just because it's seven o'clock in the morning. They are allowed to come out of the night at their own pace.

I go in quietly and sit down at her bedside as she sleeps. By spending time with the dying, I have learned to keep silent vigil with those who are asleep, or in a coma, and I have discovered the pleasure of just being there, not doing anything, just being a presence, alert, attentive, like a mother watching over her sleeping baby. The psychoanalyst W. F. Bion has a nice expression to describe this sort of accompanying, which, in his view, has important calming effects, particularly on emotional anguish: He speaks of "a mothering reverie." It isn't always easy to accept a certain vagueness, to slip into an immediate, spontaneous emotional resonance with someone else. Many of the people I've met at the bedside of the dying feel themselves to be useless and ill at ease in this situation of just being there and not doing anything. Some of the staff on the unit have learned that this, too, is part of their healing. But it calls so much into question. When you have been trained to be effective and to perform, to wash twenty patients in a morning, or give an injection in less than five minutes, it takes a great deal of personal courage to accept that you can and should spend time doing absolutely nothing in the presence of someone who is dying. How often nurses are rebuked for wasting time when they follow their heart's natural instinct and give a little of their simple presence to the sick.

DOMINIQUE has opened her eyes a little and seen me.

"I'm going to die soon, Marie. I want to thank you for all the help you've given me." Her voice is so weak as to be almost inaudible. "Everything is fine now. I'm at peace." A tear is running down her right cheek. I am extremely moved, and I touch my lips to the back of her hand in a kiss that contains, I hope, all my admiration for her and all my silent joy in seeing her finally leave serenely.

❖

Now I am going to see Marcelle. All I know since the scene I saw the other day is that she has seen all her children again and that her days are calm. There's been no further question of mental confusion.

Sitting up straight against her pillow, with her white hair combed up neatly into a chignon on top of her head, she receives me like a dowager reigning over the pristine white universe of her bed. She describes the ceremony of their good-byes, with all her children and grandchildren gathered in the room, the last advice she had for some, her account of her beloved Maurice's death some years before, which she wanted her children to hear so that they would remember and know that he, too, died bravely. She tells me how the youngest grandchildren came and sat on the bed and touched and hugged her. Little Paul, who's eight years old, put his arms around her neck and said, "Granma, is it true that I won't see you again when you go away?"

And in front of her assembled family she said, "Death is like a ship sailing away toward the horizon. There's a moment when it disappears. But just because you can't see it anymore doesn't mean it doesn't exist." Could there be a simpler or more beautiful way of explaining death to a child?

❖

In the next-door room, a young woman keeps ringing for the nurse every five minutes. I've already detected a certain exasperation among the nurses and the nurses' auxiliaries. They've been bothered since morning by these continual summonses for trifles—a glass of water, a minor change of position for a pillow. No matter how available they make themselves, and how uniquely good-natured they are, there comes a moment when they've had enough. Guessing that there must be some inner distress at work here that she has no idea how to reach, Simone, the auxiliary, grabs my arm as I'm going down the corridor and asks for help.

THE YOUNG woman's name is Charlotte. She's about thirty, but already she looks so old. Skeletally thin, her face all furrowed, she stares at me with huge black-circled eyes that are filled with pain. She has the very short hair of women who have had chemotherapy and have gone bald within a matter of weeks. She has breast cancer, which has metastasized very painfully into the bones. A nurse by profession, she knows everything about her illness. And that is what's upsetting her, she tells me. She knows that she's going to die, and she can't stop thinking about all the patients she nursed year after year in a cancer ward who died in terrible suffering. She made the decision to come and die in a palliative care unit, but she doesn't believe we can give her any relief. She's getting sicker and sicker, she doesn't get out of bed anymore, and her body is so thin that it makes her ashamed. As she talks to me, she fidgets continuously and tries three times to ring for the nurse. I ask her not to do that while I'm there. I say it with a certain firmness and this seems to reassure her. I sense that she needs to feel boundaries. I also sense her mistrustfulness.

"Yes," she says, "I don't feel confident in all this. I have to be continually on the alert."

"You'll need several days to feel you can trust us enough to relax. I've got some spare time now. If you would like to tell me a little about yourself, I'll stay right here."

The offer to be heard, and of the time needed, almost always has a calming effect. Once again, this turns out to be true. Charlotte is no longer fidgeting restlessly. She starts to talk. About her husband, with whom she's spent the last ten years as a quasi-stranger. "We don't have much to say to each other." About her nine-year-old daughter, whom she's raised rather like a doll, and about the friend who is her sole confidante. Her voice sounds disillusioned. Life seems to have disappointed her. "I've become so hideous," she goes on. Last night, she dreamed about a crow. "Crows reek of death, just like me."

WHEN I leave, I'll tell the nurses that she needs to feel recognized and loved. She's just given me the key to her agitation. When children are playing in the park and go to pick up a dead bird, you say, "Don't touch, that's dirty." She believes she smells of death; she's afraid of being rejected, pushed away like some dirty thing. We have to be able to help her to see herself differently, and to feel accepted as she is.

◇

THE DOOR to room 812 is wide open. A man who's still very young—he doesn't even look thirty—is lying on the bed, his head turned toward the door, apparently waiting for someone or something.

I go in. I know this must be Paul, the one the doctor told me about, the one who's demanding that we bring on his death. It's hard for me to conceal my surprise. Paul certainly doesn't look as if he's dying. He's a big, strapping, vigorous young man, and full-bodied. He seems to have suffered none of the physical ill effects of this illness that usually ravages the body. He just looks tired, really tired, with big circles under his coolly indifferent eyes. He seems pleased that I go and sit on the edge of his bed; he looks as if he's bored.

"Who are you?" he asks in that tone of voice that you hear in almost all AIDS patients. It signals that the speaker wants to continue being a vigilant protagonist, that he or she wants to know whom they're dealing with; it's a tone I like because it tells me that there's a will to be present, and to remain the subject of one's own life.

"I'm Marie. I'm the staff psychologist." I like to introduce myself by my first name. It's a way of saying that I'm a person before I'm a listening professional.

BEING visited by a psychologist sets up different reactions. Sometimes the word itself causes fear. In some people's minds, it carries the stigma of mental illness, of madness. Sometimes people think that the psychologist either reads their thoughts or is there to go digging into the most private secrets of their lives. And so people distrust them. I've been rejected simply because of what I do. I don't allow myself to be overly saddened by this, because I know it's a question of culture. But I also know, after all these years of listening, that the important thing is to establish contact. Once trust has been established, once the current can flow, it is rare for the proferred opportunity to talk about oneself, one's fears and feelings, to be passed up.

For his part, Paul responds very positively to what I do. He comes from an intellectual milieu in which people like to talk about themselves. Knowing that there is a psychologist on the team reassures him. It means that he will be taken seriously, in what he thinks and in what he's living through.

I LEARN that it was Paul himself who made the decision to come to our palliative care unit to die. A year ago, his friend died here in another room, and it was Paul who was beside him to accompany him. That was when he promised himself to come here to die when his own time came. Life went away when his friend died. Since then, he says, it has no meaning for him. Paul stopped all treatment. When his friend died, he stopped taking AZT. Now he has neurological attacks that stop him from walking, a cytomegalovirus that has cost him the sight of his left eye, and his immunological defenses are zero. He wants nothing, *nothing*, but to die as soon as possible.

Listening to him, it seems to me that Paul is depressed but certainly not yet dying. What can I do for him but listen to the grief and despair of a man who decided a year ago not to outlive the person who meant so much to him? After stopping the treatments, he decided to sell the business he ran. Before coming into the palliative care unit, he put all his affairs in order. He's ready to die now. But his body is still capable of sustaining life for a time, life that is there and won't go away. But what remains for him? What can he do with his days?

Now Paul talks about his parents. They have come from their distant province to be with him, to accompany him. They have moved into his apartment, and they come to spend every afternoon with him. "I can't stand them anymore," he says finally, with a sob. He has given me the key to the source of his distress. I encourage him to go on.

"I never told my parents I was homosexual. They've never known anything about my life. They don't know I was living with someone who died a year ago. I have had nothing to say to them for years, and now here they are every day; they sit here and look at me sadly. We have nothing to say to one another. The hours go past in heavy silence. I pretend to be asleep. I can't go on like this!"

"It's obviously intolerable."

"You see, I would go and see my parents regularly. I talked about my work, my business. They were proud of me. I never talked about my private life. They couldn't have coped."

His words tell me how lonely he must have been. Faced with death, he clearly cannot judge to what extent he wishes he could reduce the distance he has helped create between his parents and himself, and reestablish the bond from his childhood. Does he himself know how he longs for a real rapprochement? To be able to say, "This is who I am; this is how I loved; this is how I suffered," and to feel himself accepted, taken in, loved.

Can I help him? Will he allow me to meet his parents? Would he want me to talk to them? "Yes," he says. "Try to feel out the ground about my homosexuality. I'd like to know how my father reacts. I'm very afraid of that. But you have to come and tell me right away."

It's not the first time I've been asked to be the mediator. When it's a question of working to improve understanding between people, to unblock the channels of communication, I'm happy to lend myself to the task. So I promise Paul to meet his parents and then to come and see him again. I'm barely out of his room before I meet a couple coming timidly toward me, visibly impressed by the green plants and the reproductions of paintings hanging in the illuminated alcoves that mark out the length of the wide corridor that links the twelve rooms of the unit. "It's so beautiful," the little red-faced man with the piercing eyes says to me before stopping outside Paul's room. I realize that these are his parents.

❖

NOW ALL THREE of us are sitting in one of the small reception rooms where I see families. Paul's father has put himself next to me on the sofa, while his wife is sitting as far away as possible in a corner. So he will be the partner in this conversation, and despite all my efforts to include his wife in our discussion, she will remain silent to the very end, choosing to keep herself apart, although hyperattentive to everything that is being said.

Right away, in the fashion of a man accustomed to taking charge of things, Paul's father starts interrogating me about his son's health. He obviously thinks

I'm a doctor. I explain what I do, emphasizing that Paul is also suffering psychologically and that we can try to help him together.

"Listen, we don't know what more we can do. Paul told us a week ago that he was very ill and that there was no cure. He sent us a whole pile of papers about this AIDS illness. We came right away, my wife and me, and we moved into his apartment, it's a beautiful apartment, you know," he says with a flash of pride in his eyes. "We're trying to understand what's going on, we're trying to read all these papers, it's a nasty illness, but he's got to fight it, we're here to help him, a good-looking boy like him, he can't do this to us," and then after a silence, "we keep wondering how he caught it."

"You have no idea?" I don't want to miss the chance finally to open up this subject.

"We've wondered, my wife and I, since he never got married—we wondered somehow if there wasn't some question of homosexuality."

Paul's father has dropped his voice, and his eyes, too. He doesn't dare to look at me, and a heavy awkwardness has suddenly imposed itself between us.

"Paul is suffering a great deal because he was never able to talk to you about it," I say gently.

"I just can't believe it!" says this father, floored by the confirmation of his suspicions. "It can't be true." He has put his head in his hands. I can feel his distress. Then, raising his eyes to me, he says, "I don't want him to know that we know." I try to tell this unhappy man that his son is struggling under the weight of the silence that surrounds his life, that now that he's close to death, he would like to be able to talk about himself, and his choices, or at least know that he is accepted for what he is by the parents he has tried to protect until now. I say to the father, whose eyes are now filled with tears, that his son is afraid of how he will react, and that he can surely do Paul immense good by sharing his feelings with him.

"It's out of the question," he says flatly. "I love my son. It's his life—I respect it, but I don't want to discuss it with him." Trying to find an ally, I look at the mother, unhappy and pensive in her corner. Does she not feel this could help her son? But the father sticks to his position: He will not discuss this with his son. I realize we won't get any further today. I, too, have learned to be patient. Things find their own way, at their own rhythm.

Before I leave them, I tell them Paul is waiting for me to tell him how they reacted. "He will certainly be comforted to know that you love him and that you respect his life," I say.

◇

AT THE END-OF-MORNING meeting, we discuss the tense, gloomy atmosphere that sometimes reigns in patients' rooms. We don't just receive people who are reaching the end of their lives; we receive families where ties have been unhealthy for years, and which now reveal their weakness and deficiencies. Because nothing can remain hidden when there's so little time left, and when everything that was acting as a screen suddenly looks so flimsy. When one's intimacy is rooted in another person's and one feels a deep rapport, silence can feel like a benediction. But not for those separated by a trench. For anyone who has failed to take the trouble to discover the true nature of the person who is lying there, dying, this silence becomes an abyss, or hell. What can we do? Not much.

But we also know that once we accept this powerlessness, it becomes our strength. To continue to do what one can in a context of general helplessness paradoxically has a great impact.

TO KNOW one's own limits, accept them, and continue to give what one can—a smile, one's energy for life, one's trust—can seem irrelevant, even smacking of moral piety. Yet this is a perfectly pragmatic course to take, and one that has proved its value. Everyone tries with as much humility as possible to hold to this course. It doesn't stop anyone from experiencing moments of depression or discouragement or exhaustion. What could be more natural? Who has not suddenly found a person, a gesture, even a word to help them through such moments? A voluntary worker with time to smoke a cigarette with you and just listen. A letter from a family in mourning that gives you courage; even the smile of someone who's sick, which has the power, too often forgotten, to heal the healer. At this moment, Dr. Clement is so happy because Marie-France seems to be changing her point of view. He says she's accepting the idea of spending her last moments with us. She seems to have understood the spirit of the unit and is overwhelmed by it. "I had to come here to discover that goodness does exist," she said to one of the voluntary workers who was helping her to eat dinner last night.

◆

I AM OFTEN amazed by the phenomenon of synchronicity, these meaningful coincidences and unconscious links between things. We had just been discussing that observation of Marie-France's about goodness when I got the idea of going to see Charlotte.

LIKE Marie-France, Charlotte is struggling with her own physical deterioration, and like her, Charlotte has managed gradually to blur away the sense of shame that dominated her when she arrived in the unit. The way the staff take care of her has had a lot to do with it.

This afternoon, when I sit down beside her, she cuddles up in my arms. I rock her gently.

"I'm afraid of dying. I don't know how to die. Help me, please."

I'm struck dumb. I do not know how to die, either. "I think it's easier than we think. You could say that it happens of its own accord. Maybe there's something in us that 'knows,' " I say.

She looks at me with her large eyes sunk in their dark sockets. Suddenly, she moves her hand toward my neck and takes hold of the Egyptian cross I wear, the one that's also called "the staff of life" or "the key of Isis." She wants to know what it represents. I tell her about the bas-reliefs in the royal tombs of Egypt, on which one can see the dead journeying through the underworld, holding the staff of life until they start climbing again toward the light. "Everyone has his or her staff of life, which will help to journey through death. You'll find yours, too."

． ． ．

CHARLOTTE hugs me closer. She says she feels something warm and sweet inside, a longing to love: "I feel I still have a lot of love to give."

"That's what will help you, ma cherie, you can't do much from your sickbed anymore, but you can show all the love that's inside you." Then I leave.

ON MY WAY OUT, I see that Marie-France's door is open. She is alone, sitting in her armchair. I go in and kiss her, which always brings tears to her eyes. It's been months since anyone has been affectionate with her.

"I'm happy I came here before I die. I found goodness here. I didn't believe in it anymore. But you know the most extraordinary thing," she continues in the slightly lecturing way she always has when she talks to us, and which must come from the academic world in which she grew up, "it's that I also feel the longing to be good. I'm not worth anything anymore. I want more than anything to die as soon as possible, and strange ideas keep coming up in me. For example, I tell myself I could offer up my death, and this long, painful preamble, for someone else's benefit."

"Are you thinking of anyone in particular?"

"Yes, my little autistic cousin. It's odd . . . I don't believe in God, but I tell myself that there's some kind of invisible solidarity. I would like to help him. I would like all this to have a point, all this suffering not to go to waste."

"I like the idea of invisible solidarity."

"Well, my dear," she adds, tapping my hand, "if it does exist, you can be sure that I'll help you and everyone else here once I'm on the other side."

◇

WINTER has come, with its great freezing spells and its interminable evenings, the anxieties that come with nightfall, which starts in midafternoon, requiring that we make our presence felt even more strongly. Christmas is coming, too. We know just what upheavals such an emotive festival can call up. There's the fear of not reaching Christmas, the sadness of living one's last Christmas, the anxiety of having to confront other people's emotions.

PATRICIA has started to make little presents for everyone on the team. Her daughter is in charge of all the shopping, which Patricia orders with particular care for each and every individual.

This morning, she complains that her room is cold. It's true that it faces north. The sun doesn't come in. For the first time since her arrival, she mourns this lack of light. She would like to change rooms. As this is impossible since the unit is full, Simone offers to put her in a wheelchair and take her to sit at the end of the hall, near the big south window. Patricia, who's getting weaker day by day, is full of energy this morning. She will go and enjoy the sun this way, but first she wants Simone to help make her beautiful. This morning, it will be a chignon with some orchids stuck into it, and she must have color on her cheeks, and lipstick. She wants to make a real effect.

. . .

THIS longing for sun and sparkling effect when winter comes suddenly makes me think of the maple leaves I saw last autumn in Quebec. Feeling their imminent death, the leaves deck themselves in their most magnificent red, a kind of gauntlet of insolent defiance thrown down in front of winter, before they themselves fall. Is Patricia having an intimation of her own death? Here she is, so moving in her beauty, being gently pushed along by Simone, who's singing:

> *"When you walk through a storm hold your head up*
> *high and don't be afraid of the dark.*
> *At the end of the storm is a golden sky*
> *And the sweet silver song of a lark. . . ."*

Pierre, Patricia's husband, is reading the paper as he sits waiting for her right in front of the large window, which is bathed this morning in winter sun. He looks up and his eyes fill with tears at the vision of his beautiful, glowing wife, so close to death.

❖

A YOUNG boy of twelve, frail, sad-faced, is now coming timidly down the great pink corridor to the room at the end, next to the window where Patricia's exhausted body is soaking up the last warmth of the sun while her husband, sitting a little to the side, watches her the way you watch someone who's going away forever, with infinite grief. The little boy makes a slight movement of his lips in greeting, then knocks gently on the door to room 774.

75

. . .

MARIA, her face pallid, her burning dark-circled eyes fixed on the door, is waiting for her son's visit. She arrived a few days ago in appalling condition. Her lymphoma has been advancing at terrible speed.

Her left leg was amputated, but now the hip is affected and the intolerable pain has led her to ask for the help of the palliative care unit. So she's been receiving morphine for the past few days, and this respite allows her to sleep. Maria takes a lot of refuge in sleep. One can understand. She knows that the battle is lost. Turned in on herself like a mortally wounded animal, she's waiting for death. Yesterday, she asked the chaplain to bless her amputated leg, which she still feels with the ache of what we call "phantom limbs." Strange request. Last night, she asked that the nurse say some prayers out loud to help her to go to sleep. Chantal rocks her to the rhythm of the Hail Marys, which they recite together quietly. It is precisely because she is able to ask us for what she needs, in her extremity, that Maria moves us so much.

WHEN I went to see her, it was her twelve-year-old son she wanted to talk about. She cried a lot. Her worst agony is leaving behind this child whom she will not see grow up, whom she will not be able to protect or console when he's hurt by life. Her heart is more wounded by this than anything. I also have a son this age, and her grief undoes me. There are moments when I feel that there's nothing more I can do that's of any use, that I'm drowning too. We wept together, because I didn't know what else to do. Strangely, that's what sometimes helps. So she talked to me about Pedro. She asked me to help him, talk to him.

"He's so brave when he comes, and so gentle. He says to me, 'Come on, little Mama, courage.' He tries to hide his sadness; I can see it quite clearly. I'd like to manage to talk to him, tell him that I'm going to die but that I'll always be there to watch over him. But I can't say it to him—I can't."

I promised Maria that I would tell her son what she'd just said to me, that she could count on me. It seemed to do her some good. It was all I could do.

◇

MARIA died last night. Her body is still lying in her room this morning, because the stretcher-bearers have not yet come to fetch it. I went to her side when I arrived this morning. She looks incredibly young now that her face no longer carries the marks of her suffering. She looks touchingly beautiful. It may sound strange to describe a corpse this way. Yet some inexplicable quality is emanating from her, some trace of what she was, which wants to linger still, like an enduring perfume perhaps. Certain traditions hold that the soul remains for a time near the body. Somehow, it seems possible to believe this. This morning, I renew my promise to her to talk to Pedro. I have had no chance to do so yet, but I saw him in one of the little family rooms, crying in his father's arms.

NOW I'M SITTING beside the boy. He's not crying anymore. His face is serious and his eyes are the eyes of someone who has grown up too quickly. I talk to him about his mother. He has to know how much he helped her. She told me so. He was her joy and support. Now big silent tears have begun to run down his cheeks. He also must know that she had a very deep faith and that she absolutely knew that death would not separate them in any meaningful way—she wanted him to know that she would always protect him, whatever the circumstances. She absolutely wanted him to be sure of this. She would be there, because "love is stronger than death," as she always said. She would not let him fall. It was her last promise.

THE CHILD listened to it all with absolute attention, then thanked me gravely. I went and had a coffee. I was shaken to the core.

◇

THERE are days when the team meeting really performs its role as safety valve. That's when the emotional surges one or another of us has undergone have taken their toll. You can try all you like to establish the right emotional distance, but sometimes you go under. But doubtless it's also the price you pay for not becoming desensitized, for simply remaining human.

Today the team is rather like a single, large, sad, worn-out body. Maria's death affects more than one of us. How could we not identify a little with a woman of her age? How could we not be shaken by her grief at having to die too soon? We find it hard to banish her son's sad little face from our minds. And then, everyone senses that Patricia's time is coming, too.

She's beginning to sink into that particular kind of unconsciousness that we call a waking coma, because she still responds to the sound of her name or to a touch, but it's already the first signal of her impending departure, and the loss of communication is often experienced as a form of death.

MARIE HÉLÈNE, our ward sister, rightly observes that there's more than just sadness to the unit. Indeed, Charlotte has been transformed the last few days, starting from when she felt the wish to live out her goodness. She no longer seems to be in any emotional distress. She's gentle and sweet with everyone around her. Marie Hélène reports that her family is amazed by the change in her. Nobody had seen her in this light before. A voluntary worker who sat with her last night reports that she dozed off for a moment next to Charlotte. Her head slipped onto the bed. When she woke up, Charlotte was stroking her hair and saying, "You're so tired, my dear."

❖

LAST night, while talking with some friends, one of them made me realize that the patients in our unit are exiles in a way. They have left almost everything and they're preparing to disappear. Perhaps that's why they surprise us so, and surpass themselves.

I'M STILL thinking about this in the meeting when Dr. Clement announces the arrival of a most remarkable young woman. She has ALS (Lou Gehrig's disease) the neuromuscular degenerative disease that in its final phases involves almost total paralysis. The young woman can still move her eyelids and flex her left forefinger. Everything else is paralyzed. But beyond this utter dependence, our new patient possesses, according to her dossier, a most unusual force of character and a truly staggering willpower. We also learn that she has two adolescent children and is surrounded by a whole chain of friends. Her son had the idea of fixing up a lever attached to her word processor, and thanks to her left index finger, miraculously exempt from paralysis, she can write, laboriously selecting on the screen the letters she needs. Dr. Clement's presentation is met with silence. Each one of us is reckoning up the challenges involved in accompanying this particular patient. It is the first time that the unit has taken in a patient as dependent as this one. We will have to learn how to communicate with her, Dr. Clement explains. She says yes by closing her eyes, and no by keeping them open. Of course, she cannot call anyone. The only sound she can make is a poor little whining noise. So we'll have to organize a more or less permanent presence at her bedside. When she needs something, she makes her little noise. Her friends have made up a series of pictures that will be attached to the head of her bed. Each picture contains a series of questions that have to be systematically asked about her needs. Would she like to change position? Would she like music or to be read to? Would she like to be set up at her word processor so that she can write? She usually answers with her eyes, except when she's tired and her eyelids can no longer respond. Then she's left to rest. The doctor continues calmly to enumerate the instructions. The silence is getting more and more onerous. Will we be up to this? Everyone is silently asking the same question. Now comes the crucial instruction: She must never be positioned with her head facing forward, or she will not be able to breathe. Her head must always be turned to one side, and moved from one side to the other every one and a half hours. The young woman's name is Danièle.

◇

AT THE HOSPITAL of Good Help, Patrick is feeling better. His Kaposi's sarcoma has stabilized and the whole team is encouraging him to go home for Christmas. But from the moment this idea was first put to him, he's been running a fever, with quite high temperatures. So a series of tests is ordered. However, our pretty chief of staff, who is psychologically very acute, suspects some form of psychosomatic resistance. She called me on the phone about this, and here I am beside Patrick, whose eyes are bright with fever. What does he think about going home for Christmas?

"I'd like to go home, you know—I'm sick of the hospital—but I don't know why, the whole thing upsets me," he says, gesturing toward his midriff. "Every time I think about it, I feel a lump right here."

"So what do you think about?" I ask, sitting down on the edge of his bed and gently laying my hand on the part of his body that he says is hurting him.

"I think about my friend Bernard, who died at Christmas. I didn't understand that he was going to die. I couldn't make myself accept it. I blocked his death completely." Big tears run down his cheeks as he makes this admission.

"So that's a big lump of guilt in there," I say, gently rubbing his pain.

He needed to make this confession and talk at length about Bernard. He also thinks that this Christmas could well be his last.

"Isn't that a good reason to spend it with your family, and to allow your mother and brother, whom you've drawn so close to again these last few weeks, to take care of you? Even if you couldn't do it for Bernard, won't you allow your brother to do it for you?" I feel that my argument may be striking home.

Let's hope his fever starts to drop.

❖

THE ROOM next to Patrick's now has a new arrival, an utterly emaciated young man. He has arrived from a large unit for infectious diseases, where they have been trying in vain for the last month to stop his constant diarrhea. His biological tests are catastrophic, his immune defenses zero. He talks about his health quite calmly, with no great illusions. If he asked to change hospital units, it's for strictly humanitarian reasons. He cannot bear this sense of just being a room number, or reduced to a pathology: "the cyto in number twelve." The way the doctors do their rounds is also unendurable to him.

"They arrive in your room ten at a time. A neutral handshake, if you're lucky, then they're surrounding you and discussing the treatment as if you weren't there anymore. The chief doctor asks the matron how often you've dirtied your sheets, if you're sleeping okay, if you're vomiting, all this over your head, as if you were defective. The interns stare vaguely out of the window so as not to catch you looking at them anxiously. Then someone mutters something incomprehensible about experimenting with another treatment, and the whole crew turns on its heels, without one single person having had the common decency to sit with you for a few minutes and ask you how you're getting through all this."

HE HEARD people talking about the little unit where they treat people, not illnesses. That's all he asks now. He doesn't expect great things from medicine; he expects a great deal of people and of the quality of their care, for his body is going piece by piece. It would be more accurate in his case to say it's dissolving. This body he took such care of, was so proud of, a body that gave pleasure to him and to others, made him tempted to kill it by swallowing as many sleeping pills as would do the trick. But he's past that now. He has rediscovered his old taste for meditation.

He spends long hours with his eyes closed, stretched out in silence on his bed, or sometimes listening to New Age music, which relaxes and calms him. While the doctors still have hopes of treating the intestinal infection that is emptying him day by day, he seems to know that death is close. All he asks is to be allowed to prepare for it in his own way.

I've often observed that patients have a better awareness of their state than we have, and a better knowledge of what they need. Taking heed of them sometimes makes all the difference.

◆

CHRISTMAS has arrived. At the far end of the gallery that forms the unit, the tree sparkles in all its garlands. At its foot, a mound of little presents is waiting to be distributed. Among them are the ones Patricia made with such gentle thoughtfulness, and which she will not be able to give us herself, because she died this morning, after three days in a coma.

MY HEART doesn't feel sad, just very grave, as it always does at the death of anyone I accompanied to the very end. A life is over. I feel glad I was able to help her in the difficult times, like the day she realized she was not going to get better. I feel grateful to her for showing me how I could be of help and how one can preserve one's love of life and one's high spirits in the face of suffering and of knowing oneself diminished. And I feel how terribly fragile life is.

THIS afternoon, the team gathers and we stand together around Patricia's body. She looks as if she's asleep, with a white orchid in her hair, so young in death. Her daughter and Pierre, her husband, cannot take their eyes off her. She's beautiful, as beautiful as she was before the illness that left its mark on her face. And now she's lying straight under the light sheet, as proud-backed as a queen, whereas she always used to be curled up in her bed, as is everyone who suffers pain for months on end, until they are forced into a permanent hunch. Chantal, the night nurse, has taken the trouble to bind Patricia's legs tightly from the top of the thigh to the knees. It's her particular way of restoring what she perceived as Patricia's inner uprightness. She tells us later that it was a last gesture of affection and homage.

So we're all gathered around her, listening to the psalms the minister is reading for her and for us. "The Lord is my shepherd; I shall not want." Each of us meditates on this promise of a life in which nothing will be lacking. Moments such as this bring us back to ourselves. One day we, too, will have this mystery; none of us knows where or when. But perhaps we'll think back to this one or another, and to this grandeur of a certain kind in the face of death—a quality that is rooted in acceptance. Perhaps the deaths of people we have accompanied will help us, too, when the moment comes.

Patricia's daughter asks me shyly to sing the "Ave Maria" that I sang at Patricia's bedside a few days before she died. It was the evening she went into the agonies of her final coma. Thinking that she might die from one moment to the next, I had stayed with her. It was late, eleven o'clock perhaps, when suddenly Patricia came out of her coma and said, "Sing for me." I began to sing the "Ave Maria" she loved, the one from her childhood, and Patricia accompanied me with a little trembling movement of the lips, encouraging me to keep singing with a faint "Yes," repeated with a movement of the head from side to side. I must have sung for an hour like that before she fell asleep.

IT'S THAT memory that gives me the strength to start the song now, in front of the whole team, although there's a lump in my throat. A nurse starts to cry, and another puts an arm around her. There is a great deal of tenderness in the room, the shared emotion that passed day by day between Patricia and those who took care of her, and between Patricia and her family; it moves you in your bones.

ONE BY ONE, we leave the room, promising on this Christmas Eve to add a little extra gentleness to the lives of those around us. My resolution today is to say "I love you" more often to everyone who matters to me.

I AM HUDDLED in bed. Double-aggravated conjunctivitis in both eyes. The pain and the impossibility of opening my eyes force me to stay under my feather bed. But now another pain is working its way to the surface. I have just realized that this infection broke out on the anniversary of my father's death. There I am, trapped in bed with this thought, when suddenly all the emotions come flooding up in a huge wave and break over my head. I can't stop crying. I'm crying all the tears I couldn't cry when he died. All that buried grief. Seven years ago, I held in my pain. I wanted to behave well. I took everything onto me, just like so many people in mourning, because there is no place in our society for people who weep over the loss of someone they love. No one helped me to bring out my grief then. If the bereaved are depressed, it's considered abnormal and they're sent to the doctor for antidepressants. People try to amuse you or take your mind off it all. In other words, you're being told your grief causes fear in others.

But the need at these moments is surely precisely

to talk about the person who is no longer there and to review the circumstances of their death. Certainly this will make you cry. It's good to cry in the presence of your friends, to feel that it's possible, just as it's good to talk together about the times you spent with the person who's gone. It's good to talk about your regrets, your remorse about whatever makes you remorseful, and even your anger. All this is what helps in the work of grief, that strange inner work toward detachment that permits you finally to wake up one day, liberated and full of energy for life.

UNDER my feather bed, blind for a few days, I cannot stop thinking about everything I inherited from this deeply private man. All the joys, the remembered gestures of affection, all the little signs of his great generosity—everything that lit up my childhood rubs elbows unhappily with the profound melancholy of his last years, his sadness at getting old, which I didn't know how to alleviate. All this fills my heart. I realize I have not mourned. Perhaps I'm doing it now. Only today can my body finally give expression—with my eyes as intermediaries, all fire and water—to the violence it experienced in the suicide of my father.

I understand now that there's no economizing in the work of grief. Whatever you set aside now bursts out later, when there's another death to mourn or another anniversary.

And I also know now, because I'm going through it, how utterly alone the bereaved are. Will they find people around them who can help them articulate their sadness or perhaps the anger into which they are plunged by the death of someone they love, particularly if the death is brutal and sudden? Will they find someone to listen to everything they would like to say to the person who is no longer there to hear them? I learned a long time ago that whatever was left unsettled with someone close to you before that person's death must be settled afterward, under pain of being crippled by unresolved grief. When dealing with other people, I've often urged them to start an interior dialogue with the one who has gone, to talk to the dead.

❖

CONTACT with Paul is hard right now. There is enormous anger in him, which he can express only by turning it on himself, refusing to eat, shutting himself off, his eyes closed, his large body curled into a ball, turned away toward the window. The only way I have found of maintaining any contact with him is to suggest that we smoke a cigarette together. It is the one thing that rouses him to sit up in bed and agree to talk a little.

"I want to get out of here; I want to be left alone." There is violence in his eyes and in the way he says this to me.

DESPITE the conversation I had with his parents, there is still a heavy silence between Paul and them. Nothing has gotten said. His father seems to have stuck to his position. So the afternoons have become a torture. Once the daily banalities have been exchanged, deathly silence falls. And Paul has no other way out than, effectively, to play dead. Eyes shut, he waits with an immobility that is terrifying for the hours to pass, until his parents at long last go home.

I REMIND Paul of what was said when I talked to his father. "Why don't you take the initiative? You can't go on like this; it's unbearable! Your parents don't dare to bring it up, but you can help them. Do it yourself." I'm deliberately pushing him a bit, because what matters is Paul, and the quality of life he can have in the time that is left. And he knows he cannot die without having had this conversation with his parents.

"No, I can't. I've never talked about my own life. I've always avoided it. I can't start now."

And I realize that his confession probably won't happen.

BUT PAUL has affirmed something about himself in saying this; he has spoken in the first person, and I am curious to see the effects in him of taking this stance. The very next day, I hear that Paul has called a cousin whom he's been very fond of for years. He has asked her to come and see him. She's the one he wants to talk to about his life, to confide in. That's his choice.

❖

IT'S COLD. I'm climbing the rather run-down staircase of a building near the place de la Bastille. This is where Patrick lives. The door on the second floor is ajar. I go in and say hello to a young man who's busy in the kitchen. In a few moments, I learn that he's the home help. For relatively low pay, he comes for several hours every day to do all the domestic things that patients who are being cared for at home can no longer do for themselves. He's young, makes no secret of his homosexuality, nor of his involvement with people who have AIDS. Patrick, when I join him in his room, praises this young man's kindness and willingness. Without him, Patrick couldn't stay at home. He tells me how hard it was to come back to the apartment and to admit how helpless he's become. He spends three-quarters of his time in bed, in pain. Sometimes he uses his crutches to get himself into the living room, which has also become his workshop.

"Come, I'll show you my two latest designs," he says.

Leaning on me, he takes me into the other room. The effort it costs him is so great that he collapses onto the sofa. The tears come of themselves. I sit beside him and take him in my arms. "It's too much. I can't do it anymore. I can't see where I'm headed. How can I go on living like this? The illness is invading everything and pulling me down. I try to resist and tell myself that I have to hang on tight and come out of it. But I keep thinking about Bernard's death. It's taking me over."

"You know, anyone can think about their own death. It doesn't mean they're going to die right away." I'm trying to make him feel that he can both talk to me about what he's really thinking and go on fighting to stay alive.

He seems a little calmer, and he gets up and pulls me over to a big worktable. On it are the designs for his two latest creations: two candlesticks in the shape of angels. He has christened them Love and Hope.

◇

THE FIRST days and nights that Danièle is with us are a trial for the whole team. You can feel a muffled, pervasive anxiety. Even if not expressed, there is the fear of doing the wrong thing, the fear of misunderstanding the needs of this touching young woman. Danièle is clearly doing everything she can to put us all at ease. It takes her no time at all to seduce every one of us.

I HAVE just introduced myself to her and offered my help. She received me with a smile in her eyes; then she closed them. I know that this means yes. Would she like me to move her to her word processor? With the help of a friend who's also there with her, we lift her up a little in bed, with her head to the left, where the screen is, and her finger on the lever. The conversation begins.

"It's a difficult illness," she begins. "Communication is at heart of everything, central axis of life. The virus's stopping me from communicating is fatal." The only thing that would endanger her completely, she says, is being cut off from her friends. She goes on slowly, patiently. Watching the screen from beside her, it's a test of my patience, too. The young woman says she's condemned to "delayed speech." No more seductive conversation, flashes of wit, the little running commentary that establishes a complicity. No more long speeches. "The words are slow and come hard; I can't give them any shading with my voice, or hands, or mimicry, but I gain other things." Danièle says she can no longer hide behind words; she's lost her armor. "I know how hard this is for people around me. No charming preliminaries that let you exercise authority without seeming to do so. I have to put cards on the table, say 'I don't like' or 'I don't want.' This kind of speech is more abrupt and stiff, but it's also without artifice, and so more honest."

DANIÈLE IS showing signs of tiredness. I thank her for the effort she's put into talking to me; she asks me to come back tomorrow. She wants to talk about living with what she calls "this virus."

"I created my illness as a response to being abandoned. Cunning! But now I have proof that people love me, and I want to live, but my virus won't listen."

AFTER this first contact, the friend who's watching over her asks if we can talk. We use the time while Danièle is being washed by the nurses' auxiliaries to go and chat in one of the little reception rooms in the unit. Christiane is one of Danièle's colleagues from work. They both teach physics at a special school in the suburbs of Paris. When the first signs of the illness declared themselves, Christiane drew closer to her colleague and they became friends.

Several months ago, in a letter she was writing to her sister, Danièle touched on the question of the prognosis for her illness. Everyone had been wondering how she saw things. But now her circle realized that she believed she would get better. She said that doctors had given her to understand that a cure was possible.

"I'll let you hear all the voices inside me that are murmuring the same refrain; you choose which one you like best," she wrote.

"First there's the medical voice: It's a slow virus; it moves in, rules for a time, then goes away. Its third phase is long-drawn-out, because the regeneration of myelin takes time. Science does not know how to heal, but we have to admit it knows how to observe. I should add that I've heard this same thing more than once, so why not believe it?

"Next there's the experience I have every day in the privacy of my own body. Laugh if you feel like it—but I feel in very good health! Everything is working fine—except for my outer layer! All my organs are running like clockwork. Thank you very much! I know that seen from outside, it all looks quite different: no sound, no movement, like an unstrung puppet with arms and legs as thin as a skeleton, so it all reminds you of death. I often wonder who it's worse for: me·or everyone else.

"Then there's the voice from the unconscious. Mine's the voice of a garrulous old man in the night. Whether he disguises the virus as a bunch of implacable German soldiers (against whom I can do nothing but hide) or whether he makes it into a little white worm polluting the water in a swimming pool, he hasn't killed me yet! Quite the contrary, I've had several dreams about getting better, and they all have symbols of birth in them; so here's the message: Prepare for a christening, and not for a funeral."

CHRISTIANE is clearly puzzled. Even if this letter demonstrates everything that is helping Danièle to

93

stay alive—the belief in her cure, her humor—she finds it difficult to support Danièle in this project, knowing that the situation is irreversible and that death is certain.

"It is impossible to live without hope. Let's allow her to discover what she needs to know in her own time and in her own way. Maybe this conviction that she will get well is the way she has to go."

◇

THIS morning, the whole unit is bubbling with excitement. François Mitterrand is coming—on a private visit. The president of France is interested in our method. He encourages it and keeps track of how we're doing. I've had many chances to talk to him about it over the years at private functions. I am not part of any of his intimate circles, either political or personal, and our original meeting was quite by chance. A few words exchanged, followed by letters, led us to the rare form of intimacy (and the more precious for that) born of the discovery by two people that they share an interest in subjects that are taboo. In our case, the subject is death.

I'VE ALWAYS despised the way that journalists write from time to time about the attractions of this serious topic for the president. Some of them go so far as to say he has a morbid interest in everything to do with death. Evidently, they have understood nothing about the place this interest occupies in the complex, paradoxical nature of this man who, like the wise men and mystics of every age, has daily thoughts of his own death and has treasured memories of all those he once knew and loved.

If I share with him a daily habit of reminding myself that we are all mortal, I also share his tendency to try to analyze the agony that weighs on the lives of our contemporaries because death has been banished from our thoughts and our awareness.

There are not many people with whom he can raise this concealed topic. We live in a world that is terrified by death and hides its dying. We know the vacuum that forms around the dying, or around those who mourn their death. President Mitterrand never fails to visit a sick friend. In our talks, I've often felt the outlines of his very private sense of compassion, which few people notice in him because he keeps it so carefully hidden.

HE WANTED to pay us an informal visit this morning. The press has not been informed and the management of the hospital kept it a secret until the very last moment. It is a mark of his curiosity about this place where death is neither played down nor played up, simply accompanied, and which is not a house of death but of life.

Several of the patients have said they would like to meet the president, particularly Danièle. The team will therefore receive him in the main salon of the unit; then he will be taken to the patients' rooms.

ELEVEN A.M. The president comes through the double doors under the sign that says PALLIATIVE CARE UNIT. He's accompanied by his personal security, by his chief cabinet officer, by a former minister who's a presidential counselor, and by his personal physician, who has played an important role in the creation of this pilot unit. He is visibly impressed by the arcaded hall around which the family sitting rooms and patients rooms are arranged. I have never been sure why this corridor should give off such a feeling of quiet peace. Is it the architecture that evokes the calm of a cloister, or the soft salmon pink ceiling, or the light diffused by the large window at the very end of the row of columns? The president comes to a stop for a moment. Now he's shaking lots of hands, because everyone is here, doctors, nurses, voluntary workers, all honored by this mark of his interest in work that is so little recognized in a world in which the care and attention given to the individual carry no value.

SITTING in the large room reserved for patients' families, he's listening to a brief presentation by the chief of the unit. He listens attentively; this is why he has come. He wants to learn from us, from our experience and contact with suffering and death. He is here first and foremost as a humanist. Everyone feels how straightforwardly he establishes contact with this person and that, asking questions, reacting to the answers, mixing with the enthusiastic group of nurses, who leap to defend the quality of their work, not wishing to miss this unhoped-for opportunity to convince the head of state of the need for some public recognition of what they do. The atmosphere is lively. The topics jump from how behind France is in the treatment of pain to the lack of training for doctors, the general level of denial of death, and the lack of preparation of hospital personnel to accompany patients when "there is no more we can do."

The president is moved by the nurses' energy and passion, as he murmurs on our way to Danièle's room.

DANIÈLE has her face turned toward the window, so the president goes around to the other side of the bed. I see his face fill with awkward emotion at the sight of this physically frail young woman alone in her utter defenselessness, but with her eyes full of vitality, fixed on this intimidating visitor, who loses all self-assurance and turns to me for help.

"THIS is Danièle, Mr. President. Danièle cannot speak, but she can answer our questions by moving her eyelids."

"I have come, madame," he begins—and the word *madame* is said with such respect that Danièle begins to blush. She's alert to the inflection in his voice, which tells her how deeply he acknowledges what she is living through. "I have come to learn what is done in this unit to take care of you, and I'm happy to see how much attention is paid to the individual."

His eye falls on the many pieces of paper covering the wall above her bed.

The president is truly fascinated: "And you always find out what's wrong?" There's a flicker of sadness in Danièle's eyes, which does not go unnoticed by the intuitive man watching her. No, she must bear her solitude; we don't always understand what's the matter when she calls. I know I've sometimes found her in tears, then taken her in my arms, knowing that bodily contact was all I could offer for her immense loneliness.

Disconcerted, the president puts his hand over Danièle's and pats it gently. Now he's looking at her word processor. I explain how Danièle uses it and how useful it is for us in knowing her thoughts and needs. I also say how much Danièle helps us take care of her by her zest for life, her wit, and her intelligence.

"Courage!" he says as he lifts his hand away, and Danièle looks at him with her eyes full of laughter. I know her a little now, and I know the visit has made her happy.

"SHE LOOKS so serene," the president whispers to me as we go back into the hall. "She certainly has enormous strength of character."

WE'VE HARDLY left the room when he's surrounded by a swarm of nurses. "Your patients don't look as if they're in pain, nor are they agitated. How do you do it?" Laughter. What can they say? "Your own good spirits must have something to do with it, no?"

THE HEAD of the unit now leads the president into another room. It belongs to a Portuguese patient I haven't yet met. He's lying peacefully in bed, his hands folded on his clean pajama jacket, and he has a pair of immense black mustaches that curl up in points toward his cheeks. Receiving the president of France is an honor he could never have imagined for himself. This is what he says to the president, who asks him lots of questions about his twenty years as an immigrant worker in France. The man also says lots of complimentary things about the unit and the care he is receiving. He seems to want to give testimony in a very flattering way. It's the last task he's set himself, and he performs it with great seriousness. It's his way of thanking us.

"Is this man really dying?" the president asks as we leave the room. He wants to know how long most patients spend in the unit. "Less than three weeks?" He's clearly astonished. Like many people, he probably has quite a frightening idea of what a dying person is like. Can such a person live out the last days lying quietly in bed, without apparent pain?

The president's surprise is the greatest compliment he could pay us.

"What is the secret of all this calm?" he asks as he moves toward the exit, for it is time for him to leave us, as well as all these men and women whose only secret is that they turn to one another for support and never try to cheat death.

SOMETIME before this visit, the president spent a long lunch talking with me about what may make for the unique quality of palliative care units such as ours. The healers' motivation and their own personal journey mean that they have begun with a way of thinking about life that integrates death instead of excluding it. The president said, "We are each in a plane that will finally crash into a mountainside one day. Most people forget this. I think about it every day, but perhaps that's because I can begin to catch a glimpse of the mountain out of the window."

I told him that this awareness of their own mortality is the foundation of the philosophy of people who choose to work in units that serve the terminally ill. We also talked about the dread, which is not so much the fear of dying as of meeting oneself face-to-face and seeing how one has lived one's life. I gave him Maurice Zundel's *The Experience of Death*. He read it and liked it, and memorized one phrase: "The only thing that dies is death." We do not busy ourselves with death, but with life, and maybe that is the secret of the staff's calm: They know that death is a mirror that reflects one's life. They also know from experience that the people who feel they have lived life fully and intensely, who leave a density of experience behind them, are ones who suffer no metaphysical anguish.

WE ALSO talked about time, and the relationship between time and inner calm. I told him how I'd observed a kind of suspension of time in people who do not have very much longer to live. We talked about Stefan Zweig's "hours that do not die," when one experiences a presentiment of what eternity can feel like. Maybe the secret of people who care for the dying so calmly is that they are able to experience eternal time within everyday time? To become ever more attentive and aware—of themselves, of other people, of the world? To savor every moment of being alive? To know when to stand still and listen to the soft rustling of existence?

That's when the president said, "One always

finds out too late that the miracle and the moment are the same."

THE PRESIDENT has said good-bye to the team, with some final words of encouragement for our work and assurances that he would certainly discuss in the appropriate quarters what he had seen here.

In the elevator going back down to the ground floor, he murmurs, "These women, such light in their faces . . ."

It's his last remark before leaving. Back up in the unit, happiness seems to be floating in the air. The president's interest and empathy have touched everyone. And Danièle? When I go into her room, I find her at her word processor. She's started to write out her reactions. "May I read?" She blinks her eyelids for me to come and look.

"The pink eminence seemed more moved than the gray eminence." And she adds, "I wanted to tell him, It's not as bad as all that!" So typical of Danièle, full of humor. At Christmas, she was visited by Cardinal Lustiger when he came to say Mass with the unit. He's her gray eminence.

"It's not so bad" coming from a young woman who's close to death stays with me for a long time, one of those pearls of wisdom that come my way from time to time, leaving me the richer.

◊

AT THE GIVEN time, I go to Danièle's bedside. Despite her total loss of autonomy, she manages in her own way to remain mistress of her time and her affairs. She knows how to say what she wants and when she wants it.

Her dark eyes are full of intelligence and control, a strange impression in this poor, frail, vulnerable body.

"Let's talk about living with your 'virus.' It's a good way for me to get to know you."

Danièle begins to tell the story of her illness. The "virus" broke into her life in stealth, like a burglar, so quietly that for a long time she didn't know it was there. Then it began to show the first, almost imperceptible signs of its presence. She remembers the first surprises: Although she often smiled as she spoke, suddenly she noticed she could no longer do both at the same time. She had to choose. Then her voice began to change, or rather, to disappear. She had trouble pronouncing certain consonants, and she often got lost in her sentences. That convinced her to consult a doctor. It was an ordeal.

"You see, I was the only one who suspected. . . . Saying it out loud was giving a shape to the enemy, granting it the right to occupy my life. It was a declaration of war against the . . . unknown."

Danièle became acquainted with anguish. She had an intuition of how serious her illness was, at a time when no one else even knew she was ill at all. There was also the fact that her illness had never been named. What is more frightening than the thing with no name? Which is why Danièle named it "this virus."

I understand better now. The doctors must have avoided telling her that it was ALS. It would then have been easy for Danièle to find out for herself that this degeneration is irreversible. All she knew was that it was something neurological. She talks about how strange it was.

"No pain, just odd little things going wrong. Things I'd always done without thinking were suddenly impossible; on the other hand, muscles I'd never used suddenly began to twitch. . . . I was no longer in charge of myself."

I'm worried that Danièle is wearing herself out. I suggest that we stop now and continue tomorrow. But she seems to want to go on. I can feel a fierce will in her.

As if she had read my thoughts, Danièle warns me that behind her apparent strength she feels terribly weak sometimes. For a long time, she pushed away her own mental torment; then one day the dam broke.

"I've never gone through anything remotely like that: Screams were coming out of my chest, loud, raucous, uncontrollable screams, and I thought, The children will hear. And *IT* kept screaming. My whole body shook and fought against the paralysis."

Now Danièle can no longer even scream or struggle. All she can do is let the tears fall.

Lots of friends are now arriving in her room. She's obviously much loved.

As I leave, I know that we have much to learn from her.

◇

STANDING in the unit kitchen, sipping my coffee, I think about the mysterious passage that has brought me here, dressed in a white coat, ready to start a day of trying to use my presence to support patients and their families. I have borne witness to the deaths of many people whose bodies have been attacked by illness and who have been confronted—acknowledged or not, accepted or not—with their own oncoming death. Emaciated bodies, jaundiced faces with tumorous features, behind which I have encountered people whose histories are made of the ups and downs of love and despair, and passionate efforts inconclusively ended—living people, thirsty for love and anxious not to pass on before reconnecting with their true feelings. Sometimes I have been greeted as an unhoped-for presence, sometimes rejected as an intruder. But beyond all the difficulties, all the moments when I'm lost, beyond the worries or the jolts of discouragement, there's always the surprise of feeling myself more and more alive each day, while people around me sometimes view this constant cohabitation with death as morbid. How can I stay cheerful? How can I not be depressed?

HAVING swallowed my coffee, I decide to make a round of the rooms and then go and see a new arrival, a man with a rather rare illness, a cancer of the cardiac muscle that seems to have metastasized. That's all I know as I go into Dimitri's room.

An old man with an aristocratic face is resting on the bed with his eyes closed. As I come closer, he opens his eyes, which are a very beautiful green, and I meet a gaze that instantly impresses me by its intensity. This man is able to establish immediate contact. I soon learn why.

Once I've introduced myself, he says, "Do you believe in previous lives? I'm sure I've met you before. I know you . . . unless it's because you're so like my mother. You wear the same perfume she did."

He says all this with a light Russian accent that adds to his charm. So I'm doubly welcomed, even invited to share a certain intimacy created by the memory of a much-loved mother. I sit on the edge of the bed, as I often do if the patients allow it, because experience has taught me the contact this creates is more helpful in building an atmosphere of trust and sharing than if I sit at a distance in the chair. Dimitri takes my hand firmly but gently and kisses it, putting so much heart and nobility into the gesture that I immediately feel I have the soul of a Russian princess.

"How do you feel? Is everything okay here?"

"Oh yes; I can tell I will be very well taken care of. But you see, I miss seeing nature. I miss a sense of space. I feel as if I'm suffocating."

I'm always alert to this misery. It's one that our patients admit far too rarely, but one they feel, seeing themselves confined to the shrunken world of a hospital room, their single escape a fragment of northern sky.

It's lucky that we have the big window, so often bathed in sunshine, from which you can see Montsouris Park and its surrounding houses with their brightly planted terraces. All the patients who are still mobile love to go and sit right in front of it. Sometimes, we also push someone's bed all the way down there.

So this afternoon, I suggest to Dimitri that I move his bed out to the big sun-filled window. It's so touching to see this sick man abandoning himself to pleasure, his hand placed trustingly in mine and his eyes shut as he savors the warmth of the first rays of spring sun. It's a moment of happiness for me, too, as are all those moments when one can just be there, be present, without waiting for anything in particular. I'm careful not to ask any questions, which would break the delicate, silent contact he seems to want to establish with me.

AFTER a long interval, he opens his eyes. He seems to be coming out of a dream, and he looks at me for a long time. He says again that I remind him of his mother. She died some years ago. He misses her. He tries for a moment to articulate what it is in me that reminds him of her. Then suddenly, he shares a confidence:

"I just feel very good with you, very safe, as if I'd known you for years. . . ."

I feel good in his company, too. A real contact establishes itself. I do not know how long Dimitri will live, nor if I will even see him again tomorrow, but what I do know is that I will accompany him to the very end.

It's time to end this tête-à-tête. Other patients are waiting for me. I wheel Dimitri's bed back into his room.

"Come back and see me soon."

"I promise." And he takes my hand and gives it a long kiss under cover of saying good-bye.

BACK in the corridor, I head for one of the little sitting rooms reserved for the families and close friends of patients. It's empty. I shut the door and sit in one of the armchairs, in search of a moment of quiet. One can be perfectly aware that the accompanying of the dying is a matter of bonding and of love, but every connection that is established takes us onto the threshold of an adventure involving everything we have to give. This time, too, I feel the absolute seriousness of the commitment.

❖

NEXT day, I visit Dimitri again. The room is full of people, or more precisely, full of women, with Dimitri fully at ease in the middle of them all, like a pasha. The atmosphere is full of life, and more like a social tea party than a hospital room. These women in the entourage of our new patient are all stylish forty-year-olds, with the exception of one older woman of about sixty, who is, as I discover later, his ex-wife. The tone of the conversation is light, worldly, almost offhand. These women obviously have a seductive relationship with this man—which he manipulates with happy skill. When I go to his bedside, he gestures in the same casual, worldly way. "Look, it's all perfect. This is truly a four-star hospital. I have my own official analyst. Come in, my dear, come in!" Is this the same man I met yesterday? The arrogance. The affectation! This role as king-pasha among his favorites! Refusing to play his game, I use all his visitors as an excuse to say that I'll come back later. Obviously, Dimitri is complex. Yesterday, the man I met was disarming in his sincerity, and, all things considered, rather vulnerable; today, the same man is wearing the mask of the character he's obviously played with women all his life.

❖

PATRICK is back in the hospital. With a little sad smile, he says, "I think it's going to win." We both know that "it" is death.

He can no longer get out of bed. His Kaposi's sarcoma is advancing from day to day, and Tristane had a very frank but very difficult conversation with him. There is no further hope of a cure. She can promise him that the pain will be relieved and that he will receive all the comfort and care he needs. He cried for a long time, and it helped. "I'm so disappointed" is what he said.

His mother is with him, full of love and grief. Patrick says he feels so guilty about having to die. He feels every ounce of his mother's pain. He would have wanted to spare her that. This pain that she hides when she's close to him but that he feels nonetheless, is at times unendurable.

I'VE OFTEN heard dying people talk about this particular misery that comes from their awareness of the pain they must be causing other people. Experience tells me that it can be alleviated a little if the patient can discuss the onset of death with those around him, and if they can cry together.

THIS morning, Dimitri is alone. He's finishing his breakfast. The moment we look at each other, I know that I can reestablish the contact we established the first afternoon. There is no trace this morning of the false assurance he was advertising with such swagger the other day. Sitting on the side of his bed, I ask him to talk about himself and his illness. What exactly does he know? How aware is he of the gravity of his situation? I really still do not know anything about how this man is positioning himself to deal with the ordeal he is undergoing. He doesn't try to evade, and he deals with the subject in a few short, concise phrases. "I have cancer of the cardiac muscle. I know how serious it is. I can die today or tomorrow, because the doctors have told me that my heart could stop beating at any moment." And then, as if conjuring with fate to nullify the menace he had just evoked, he says, "You know, I'm a great optimist. People are going to take good care of me here. I know that I could die, but I'm not there yet."

I KNOW where I am now: While admitting the gravity of his condition, this man who loves women and loves life is still nursing a serious hope of remission. I listen, as always, in the awareness that the time left to each individual belongs to that individual alone. Nobody can predict with certainty the answer to the deepest secret mystery in any life—namely, the hour of one's death. As if to free himself of the fear brought on by the prospect he's just named, Dimitri reaffirms his belief in reincarnation: "I'm convinced that we have more than one life. I'm certain of that." After a short silence, he asks me about what I do. He himself has taken an interest in psychoanalysis and the exploration of the unconscious. And then he asks if he can tell me a dream he had just before he came to the unit. I agree and listen more. My Jungian training, my experience with patients, and my own interests have trained me to treat these particular confidences we call dreams with the greatest respect. Because these are confidences: Every dream shared is a sliver of intimacy—part of one's most secret self—that one decides to offer up to someone else. As many so-called primitive peoples know, the sharing of a dream is a ritual. To enter someone else's dream is to tread on sacred ground, penetrating their intimacy. The unconscious is not only the reservoir of what is repressed; it also contains all our potentialities. It is a breeding ground of images and symbols that can help us in our growth.

DIMITRI tells me his dream. "I'm on a beach, dressed in armor, beautiful metal, but very cumbersome. A powerful voice orders me to go into the water. I am extremely upset, because with this armor, I will certainly drown. At the same time, I cannot avoid the obligation to go into the sea. So I go forward in great anxiety, knowing that the armor will stop me from swimming. I wade into the sea until I'm almost submerged. Just when I feel completely overwhelmed with panic, the armor suddenly opens, and I find that I am swimming, free and happy."

Whenever I listen to a dream, I do not try to interpret it. First, I ask whoever dreamed it to tell me what the dream tells him or her; then I let this resonate in my mind. Associations form themselves, which I in turn offer to set beside the dreamer's own. Sometimes they may explain things differently; sometimes they enlarge the dreamer's understanding of the dream. This enriching way of sharing a dream, while respecting the intimacy of its author and what is ultimately unknowable, is a wonderful way to deepen a relationship. Dimitri's dream tells him of a terror that will give way of its own accord as soon as he agrees to

commit himself to the waves. Coming into the palliative care unit could be experienced as entering a sea in
which one knows one will drown. And doesn't the
dream also announce a kind of miracle: being freed
from the armor, or rather, the social face he has
forged for himself like an iron mask? The sea of death
transforms itself into the sea of life; the dream says
that in living his death, he would also experience liberation and happiness.

DIMITRI is very conscious of the liberating scope of
his dream. I simply confirm very gently how much the
dream is inviting him to become truly himself, to dare
to let go of his armor, to dare to be genuine. He
doesn't say anything, but takes in everything I say,
and holds my hand in his, punctuating my words with
tiny caresses, or squeezing gently. He seems open to
suggestion, able to read the messages that have risen
to the surface. After a long silence that stretches away
like an empty beach, he murmurs, "What you say
touches me deeply."

BACK in the corridor, I think, Yes, this man is on his
way to death. Can he fulfill his dream and rid himself
of what Jung would call his *persona?* Something tells
me yes.

◆

TO TELL the story of one's life before one dies. The
telling of it is an act, and for anyone whose autonomy
is so often diminished, this act takes on its full impor-

tance. There is a need to give shape to one's life and to show this shape, which gives it its meaning, to someone else. Once the telling of it has been accomplished, the person seems to be able to let go, and to die.

PAUL would have liked to have been able to present his story to his parents. In the last days, he has had to accept the death of this hope. But as he was renouncing it, he did manage to renew the old childhood bond with his cousin, and thanks to her and to the loving way she listened, he was able to achieve the essential act of sharing the most intimate part of himself, and giving shape to his own life.

Now he can let himself go. He's "diving," in the expression used by the team—diving into the waters of death. It's precisely because he feels at peace with himself at last that he's now trying for a rapprochement with his mother. He often asks her to come closer. He claims her affection. Anxiously at first, she brought her chair closer to the bed, and when he reached for her hand, she got braver. She strokes it and cradles it a little awkwardly. He is much calmer. His father still keeps himself farther away, but he looks at his son with tears of love in his eyes. Although nothing has been said between them, they are evidently close to each other.

◇

LIFE promptly confirms the intuition I had about Dimitri. Several days later, I hear that his condition has worsened. He has been seized with fits of vomiting. Now he's very weak. When I find him lying on his bed, I'm looking at a much weakened man. But the contact between us is instantaneous and without preliminaries. Slipping my hand into his as I sit as close to him as I can, I stay like that, without the faintest embarrassment between us. He doesn't just accept the contact; he is quite frank about seeking it out. His voice is no more than a murmur. I suggest that he remain quiet.

"You're too tired to talk, but I'll stay with you for a little, if you'd like."

"Oh yes, please do, stay here. It does me good."

And then he is seized with sudden, uncontrollable nausea. In a flash, I am splattered with it, all over my hands and my white coat. The bed is in a similar state, not to mention Dimitri. In the space of a few seconds, he has gone from being a very weakened man to being a soiled patient. And in this moment, instead of giving way to the all-too-classic reaction of pulling back in shame, while simultaneously barricading oneself in wounded pride, this seductive man who is so attached to his fine bearing dares to open himself and remain in affectionate contact with me. He lets go of his armor and draws on his deepest resources to find the courage to be natural. Looking up at me utterly without pretension, he says simply, "I'm so sorry to inflict this on you."

Both the look and the words touch me to the core. A great wave of tenderness wells up in me for this man who is so wounded in his sense of self and yet finds the courage to accept things as they are. The vomit is unimportant. I don't call anyone; I organize the essentials and clean up on my own. I could summon a nurse, but it's important to make Dimitri feel really loved at a moment when his mask has shattered into a thousand pieces. Picking up a box of Kleenex, I begin to clean up slowly and carefully so that it becomes a kind of rite.

I think of the nurses' aides who perform these intimate acts all day, every day, moving beyond any feelings of repugnance because the very thought of restoring someone's dignity is enough to give them all the satisfaction they need.

Patients doubtless recognize in their eyes something of the love they once saw in their mothers'; and the way the patients are taken care of surely arouses memories of being taken care of when they were babies. If many human beings know this form of happiness in their earliest years, so that they retain the memory forever in a corner of their psyches, it is nonetheless rare that this same tenderness should be given to them again at the end of their lives. As helpless as babies, once again soiled and uncoordinated in their movements, most patients are cleaned up by the competent but most often mechanical hands of tired nurses, or the hands of friends and relatives, who are more involved, at least in principle, but ill-prepared to cope with this new relationship to those whom they once knew as self-validating and independent people. Prey to confusion themselves, both children and partners in such situations frequently find themselves embarrassed, not to mention somewhat disgusted, with the result that the patient is left alone with a feeling of shame.

RELEASING himself fearlessly into my care, Dimitri has probably enjoyed the privilege of renewing the happy sensations of his childhood.

Once the rite of cleaning is over, he pulls my face to his and holds it there for a few moments. "I love you," he suddenly murmurs, and strokes my hair. I say nothing, hear his cri de coeur without recoiling. Then I very gently set myself free.

In the past few days, I've spent long periods with Dimitri, sometimes in silence, sometimes listening to whatever this man on the edge of death wants to confide in me. He says he is touched by the kind of care he receives here, which means the way the nurses tend his body. In fact, he's discovering a human dimension he had not believed was possible. The long hours of lying immobile in bed are his opportunity to meditate on life, his own of course, but also those of the men and women who tend the suffering of others. So is there such a thing as goodness in the world? He has made his way as an engineer in the desert that is the world of business, where the only things that prevail are material interests and ego. A world in which the only values recognized are those of efficiency and income potential, and where nobody hesitates to crush anyone else on the way to achieving a goal. And now all around him are people concentrating on patients in their last days of life, giving priority to emotional connections, paying attention to the inner life of society's rejects: the sick, the handicapped, the old. Upset, he tells me how he was treated during a previous surgical procedure. Under the anaesthetic, he experienced one of those out-of-body phenomena that sometimes affect the sick. Finding himself suddenly conscious, floating above his body, he saw his own flesh on the operating table surrounded by doctors, and heard the surgeon say contemptuously, "Take it away. I don't want this one to die here." Inhuman as it may be, this remark is not uncharacteristic of a certain medical mind-set that doesn't give a damn about the person and just sees a physical organism whose terminal defection in the operating room would boost the negative statistics on patients who die during surgery. Once removed from the operating room the patient is free to die even five minutes later, because then death would be attributed to postoperative complications.

◇

DIMITRI not only failed to die; when he regained consciousness, he remembered what had been said, and he was deeply wounded by it. Listening to this episode, I find myself thinking that he has spent a lifetime treating the women he seduced one after the other with exactly the same offhandedness, taking no account of their feelings. Hearing the surgeon's contemptuous remarks, was he not redirected to his own inhumanity?

BY CHOOSING to clean him with affection, so that he can experience the fact that even when he's soiled, he's still worthy of my greatest care and attention, I have perhaps repaired his feeling of being nothing but human scrap, something rather dirty. This acknowledgment of his fundamental humanity is balm on the wound inflicted by insult.

◇

THIS morning, Patrick seems to have rediscovered some of his energy. But the end is close. He tells me that he felt himself dying last night. He thought he would not see the morning. Every time he breathed out, it was an agony, because he was so afraid he would not be able to breathe in again.

"I thought I was suffocating. You can't imagine what a relief it was to see the day shift coming on duty and knowing that I'd gotten through the hell of the night."

Patrick is filled with the happiness of still being alive and of having another day in front of him. He's smiling in a way I haven't seen him smile for a long time. It does me good. I wish that patients knew how much they help us, sometimes, just by smiling.

I'm looking at this young man who is going to die and who is smiling at me. And suddenly, he starts to interrogate me about the purpose of my life, about my work here, and about what motivates us all—me, the doctors, the nurses—to look after sick people who are about to die.

"They do something very hard," he says, tears in his eyes. "I couldn't do what they do."

He talks about the nurses. He is full of admiration for these women and men who accept a miserable salary to take care of their fellow human beings. The world has always struck him as cruel and savage, and now on the verge of death, he finds that there are people who like to do good and know how to be of help without seeming be ministering to the helpless. He's very sensitive to that. He has had time to observe the nurses all day and all night. "They know how to smile, and smiling at people has nothing to do with pitying them. It's not easy to accept being hospitalized. It means being exposed to being looked at whenever people choose. It means being subjected to other people's jargon, other people's rhythm of doing things, other people's intrusions. It's humiliating." But he also knows that it's not easy to work with physical collapse and misery, and he couldn't do it himself.

"Perhaps if people thought more about what it's like for one side to be humiliated and for the other side to have to deal with that humiliation, both sides could help each other get through it. I like to help the nurses, so I do what I can—I smile at them; I try to put myself in their place."

As Patrick suggests, if everyone tried to put themselves in the other person's place, it would all be easier. Is that not the definition of compassion? Putting oneself in someone else's place—while being perfectly aware that one isn't actually there—is not the same thing as identifying with someone else; it's also stepping back the necessary distance to be able to evaluate things: If I were in this place, how would I like to be helped?

IT'S NOT THE FIRST time I've noticed that patients on the very verge of death are preoccupied with the people who take care of them. They ask us how we are; they thank us for what we've done for them; they sometimes promise to help us, if they can, after they die. They suddenly want to know more about us.

It's as if the center of their preoccupations shifts and opens up—almost as if they are seeing the world with new eyes. This is the impression I have of Patrick this morning, and I know it's also the announcement of the end.

❖

WHEN I get home that night, I phone the hospital. They tell me Patrick is dying. His parents and brother are there.

Sometimes patients ask for me to be there with them when they die. It is a promise I will not make, because the moment of anyone's death is unknowable, and I cannot say in advance that I will be there. I also know that they won't be alone. But if I'm asked, and if I can get there, I go, even during the night.

I HAVE supper with my children and return to the hospital. It's ten o'clock and the unit is quiet. The nurse who greets me thinks Patrick will not live through the night. His room is filled with the sour odor of his rotting legs. It hits me every time I go in, but then after a few minutes, I don't notice it anymore. Patrick is there, still alive, still conscious. His mother gets up to give me her place, close to his face on the pillow. I whisper that I've come to say goodbye to her son. I tell her that he has been extraordinary and that I won't forget him. Patrick hears me. He groans a little and says my name.

"I've come to thank you for everything you've given us through your endurance. Don't be anxious. Go on your way," I say, stroking his hair with all the love I feel in this moment for this young man who is dying. "You know, it's Saint Patrick's Day today." A last kiss on his forehead and I leave the room so that he can be with his family, who are crying slowly and silently and will be there with him until the end.

◇

"I want to live this difficult passage of my life as fully as possible. Everyone knows that once you cross the desert, you reach the Promised Land."

These are the words, tapped out on the familiar screen letter by letter, that open our conversation today.

We all know now that Danièle hopes for a cure and is living her illness as a period of waiting.

"What can I learn from this strange adventure? This illness that makes me stop all the things I was so immersed in and prevents me from doing the most elementary things. What is it saying, and what didn't I know enough to hear?"

DANIÈLE has thought a great deal about the meaning of her illness. She says that it is rooted in a fear of being abandoned, a fear that she felt most powerfully as a child, and which was rearoused whenever a break in a relationship intervened to tell her that she was not the best nor the most loved. Last night, I met Danièle's twin sister, who lives in Cuba and has come for a month. To see Gisèle is to know what Danièle would be like without her illness. Young, brunette, sparkling, alert. All the qualities she now evinces in the way she is and the way she gets through things.

Gisèle told me about a letter from Danièle with an account of a childhood fantasy: "Our life lacked dramatic texture. Remember how we forced Father Camille to tell us the story of 'the poor little abandoned girl'? And along the same lines, I pretended that I would get terribly ill, which would be absolutely pathetic and would reap me everyone's total love. Who knows if my little childhood fantasy may have left some imprint, ready to spring to use when life allowed. (This is me advancing a completely naïve hypothesis about the mechanism of how the body expresses things!) Obviously, as you gathered, the scenario never got as far as death, because what joy would there have been in that?"

Danièle is laboriously picking out the letters on the screen. I bend over to look. In this position, half-lying on the bed beside her, we are very close. She says that makes her feel good.

She always wanted to be given lots of love, and now she is getting it in abundance. But it is so difficult to receive it. She talks about her family's love, and that of her friends and those who take care of her, as "a fountain from which she doesn't know how to drink," and she adds, "Perhaps you have to learn to become a little child again, humble enough to accept the gift."

And this is not easy, because Danièle was the absolute opposite: She loved to give egoistically. Knowing how to receive requires abandoning oneself, letting go, an attitude dramatically opposed to the way she's always been. Will her current journey lead her to explore this fallow ground?

"What kind of a journey is illness dragging us through?" She often refers to this idea of a journey. For her, the whole idea of going forward, of moving, is primordial. How can she live in her paralysis except by moving psychologically?

Fine-tuned and intelligent, she has decided to take up the challenge of this illness. "I can tell you my weapons: Avoid all comparisons with the past and learn to live this as a particularly long and difficult passage. You see, I don't know how many years the ordeal will last, but there are difficult lessons, and they need time."

SOMETIMES Danièle cries. Big tears run down her face, which undo us.

"I didn't let the emotion out before, but now that my virus has taken my speech and my muscles, I can't keep it in anymore."

She writes about how difficult it is just to be there without voice and without movement.

◇

SOUNDS of laughter and singing emerge from the bathroom in the unit. I recognize Simone's crystalline voice, and it sounds as if the other one is Yvonne's, another nurse's aide, who is the queen of massages.

This "bath ceremony," made possible by very specialized equipment that is adapted for the bedridden, has become a rite, a rite of pleasure.

For the aides, it's something basic. "Water allows you to touch someone, make contact; it's often joyous. We take our time; we talk, and we sing."

If your body is all numb or no longer mobile, one can imagine how good it feels to know that you are floating gently in warm water: a new and wonderful way of experiencing this same sick body, which reverts in an instant to being the locus of feeling and pleasure. Anyone who is no longer touched by someone else, as is all too often the case with our AIDS patients, experiences this bath as the ultimate restitution of themselves, an ultimate recognition. Just the other day, Paul said how much he appreciated being touched without gloves.

"In my view," says Simone, "if you are touching in order to give, there's no danger. For our own equilibrium, it's important to be able to 'give something good.' "

The door opens. I recognize Danièle on the blue stretcher. So she's the recipient of this little celebration!

I wait for the staff to get her into bed and finish what they have to do before I go to her. She's relaxed, bright-eyed, ready to write.

"Being washed can be like a party—lots of sweet smells, massage that makes you feel you're being caressed, peals of conspiratorial laughter." And then: "Talking about pleasure, how could I never have noticed that moving is one of them? Will I ever get it back, or will it always be a matter of some kind of complicated exercise? Movement is the most primitive pleasure there is—you have to undergo such ordeals to find treasures you never dreamed of."

When I left Danièle, all I wanted to do was go and run barefoot in the grass like a mad thing. Get drunk on movement! I took my car and went to the park at Sceaux. It was warm, and I realized that the days were getting longer. On the big lawn in front of the castle, I took the most immense pleasure in running, spinning in circles, feeling the warm, damp earth under my feet, and I said thank you to life and to Danièle for such a conscious flash of pure joy.

◇

WITHOUT having swallowed any medications capable of inducing unconsciousness, Dimitri has sunk into a sleep that has no explanation in medicine but which presents all the aspects of a waking coma. Although he can hear and he responds to touch, he doesn't speak and he seems to be absorbed in the depths of himself. As no conversation is possible, I decide to watch with him as much as I can, whenever my work with the other patients in the unit permits. To watch with someone in this kind of coma is certainly a most remarkable experience. You lose some of your sense of time and space. By simply being there, you have the feeling of being immersed in some eternal present.

To watch quietly and patiently with the dying has always, I think, fostered meditation on life and death, a state of prayer and of intimate dialogue with the heart of oneself, what some people call God, but which I prefer to describe as the essence of all things, ultimate reality.

The waking coma will go on for forty-eight hours. Very occasionally, Dimitri comes out of his lethargy; each time, he says something very loving. It's so moving the way this old man at the very gates of death uses every moment of lucidity to do something affectionate or to find words to tell us how absolutely happy he feels, how filled with love. "I didn't think it was possible—I feel so good," he says, stroking my arm.

ALL OF US IN THE UNIT think that Dimitri has reached the end. His family and friends are with him more often, which is how the opportunity is given me to meet them. It's his young friend Natalie who makes the first move to talk to me. Natalie teaches Russian in a high school. She met Dimitri some years ago at a gathering in the home of some members of the Russian community in Paris. She's a very cultivated, very serious young woman, as discreet and private as he is outgoing. She's certainly very different from the kind of women he's seduced all his life. Small, blond, unobtrusive, very soft-spoken, calling no attention to herself. She takes on her true dimension only when you talk to her one-on-one. Then you discover her interior strength and uncommon generosity. I learn that she's supported Dimitri during these last years, once his illness started to advance, giving him the spiritual nourishment he had always craved. Perceptively, she has noticed the particular connection Dimitri has established with me. He has told her that my calmness when I'm with him has helped him a lot. "Dimitri was so afraid of death, but since he's been here, the fear has gone," she says. She would like to have been able to bring him the peace that he seems to have found with me.

HER WORDS give me pause. Have I displaced this woman with Dimitri? She does not seem to be reproaching me with this; on the contrary, her generosity is overwhelming. What am I to Dimitri that he should offer me what would be effectively his last relationship? Aside from the fact that I remind him of his mother, am I not someone he does not have to mourn? Someone he does not have to leave? He knows nothing of me or my life, has no need to concern himself about what will happen to me after he dies; I'm a kind of human presence, out of time, able to release a flood of emotion in him. I am also someone who can just be there with him, without holding him back, without tying him down, the only person perhaps who can truly give him permission to die. We know how hard it is for those who love someone to let that person go. Despite all her wisdom and maturity, Natalie's heart is full of grief at the separation to come. When she is with Dimitri, he cannot avoid feeling the weight of this grief, even if she keeps the sadness to herself.

◇

CONTRARY to all expectations, Dimitri has regained consciousness. When I arrive in the unit this morning, I am amazed to find him quite awake, even lively. Sitting up in bed, freshly shaved, finishing a mango tea, he greets me with a radiant smile. He feels, he tells me, at the dawn of a new life. This morning, he wants to talk about what are, essentially, future plans. Have I been to Venice? No? So he'll take me there. He starts to describe it all to me, each place more beautiful than the others, the green light on the Grand Canal, the slightly mournful charm of the old hotels. He'll take me to the Danieli, of course, the most beautiful hotel in Venice, with its view of San Giorgio. He's quite excited as he talks, and there's a flush in his cheeks. I listen, aware of being made part of a dream but respectful of the surge of life and hope in this momentary reality. It is not uncommon for someone who is dying, and is experiencing what we call "the best of the last," to make plans like this. It has to do with knowing that you are going to die and yet not believing in your own death. Two contradictory thoughts go forward side by side: I know I'm going to die and Death does not exist.

Dimitri this morning knows how ill he is, knows the risk of death that is weighing on him, the more so since the doctor just left him saying, "We thought you were leaving us, the last two days." Despite this, he feels so alive that his only thoughts are about life. These are the thoughts we must accompany.

MY OWN EXPERIENCE has taught me that these plunging dives into unconsciousness that characterize the approach of death often produce an outcome of well-being, of transformation, as if some spiritual exercise were working itself out deep in the soul. I think back to Dimitri's dream: These two days and nights of apparent unconsciousness have given him a respite in which to shed his armor at last and begin to swim free.

THE CONFIRMATION of this transformation comes when I meet Sophie, Dimitri's daughter. Born of his first marriage to a woman he adored but who died very young, she was separated at an early age from her father and raised by her grandmother. Any relationship with a father with a turbulent emotional life is never simple. Sophie has been left with a muddle of frustration and admiration. She would have liked to learn who he really is, to know his true self. But he has always run away even from himself, hiding behind one mask or another. And now, after this two-day coma in which she thought she'd lost him, she throws herself into his arms and feels welcomed in a way she never has before. Their long embrace begins to heal so many past wounds.

ONCE again, this accompanying of Dimitri proves that the period right before death can allow for a significant transformation of one's very being. What Dimitri has been searching for all his life in one love affair after another is this very revelation of his own goodness, which he has found at last on the very threshold of death. Perhaps what was required was something like the episode of his vomiting for him to know that he is fully accepted and loved as a human being, and that drawing on this internal security, he can dare to be himself, in all his gentleness and love.

THE DAYS that follow are marked by this state of grace. The nurses' charts all report "a lot of affection and tenderness" in his room. No more petty games, no more playacting, but quite the opposite—a wonderful feeling of serenity. We take turns at his bedside in an unbroken chain. Dimitri sleeps a lot. The doctors don't give him very much longer. Without being aware of it, he is helping everyone around him, for it is easy to let someone slip into death once you feel at peace with him or her. His behavior in the last few days has allowed each one of us to find our peace with him.

IT'S THE DAY BEFORE Easter. I'm getting ready to go to Taizé for two days with my children. Dimitri has lapsed into a waking coma again. I kiss him and thank him for the gift of so much of his love and trust in me. He opens his eyes, full of emotion, and looks at me in a way I shall never forget. I can feel that he's happy.

HE DIED on Easter Day.

At the moment of his death, I was lying in the grass, in the sun, up in the hills above the plain of Cluny. We were having a siesta. I woke at four o'clock. Opening my eyes, I saw a beautiful spring sky. I had an image of Dimitri, and I felt a great inexplicable surge of joy.

On my way back to Paris in the evening, I decided to drop in at the hospital. That's when the night nurse told me that Dimitri had died at exactly four o'clock in the afternoon, surrounded by his friends and family. I was neither astonished nor sad; since the moment I had begun to accompany him, there had been a communion between us.

Some days later, I had to go to Venice. Arriving by train, I took a vaporetto down the Grand Canal, then got off and was walking back along the canal when suddenly I thought of Dimitri and everything he'd told me about Venice. I realized that I was standing outside a hotel and that it was the Danieli. I went into the front hall and had a coffee at the bar in silent tribute to the memory of the man who gave me the most precious task of keeping him company on the way to death.

❖

SOME time later, one of my fellow analysts, to whom I've been talking about accompanying Dimitri, expresses surprise at the extent of my emotional involvement with the patients in the hospital. He mentions the essential "therapeutic distance," that barrier that protects the patient as much as the therapist. It's a question that has preoccupied me for a long time, of course. From the day of my first exercise in accompanying someone, when I found myself at the bedside of a man bent double in agony and threatening to throw himself out of the window, I knew that I couldn't just sit in a chair three feet away from the bed and listen. All the safeguards and rigid rules of the analytic world—don't touch, don't speak—melted in a single mass. I had to move up close, listen to my own intuition, speak with my heart, lay my hands where it hurt, the way I would have done with anyone in that situation.

ACCOMPANYING someone involves engaging with that person; it is a matter of the heart. Above all, it is about one's common humanity. One cannot retreat behind one's white coat, whether one is a doctor, a nurse, or a psychologist. This does not mean, however, that there are no limits. And that everyone must remain aware of his or hers. One actually is less exhausted by a total involvement of self—provided one knows how to replenish one's reserves—than by the attempt to barricade oneself behind one's defenses. I have often seen for myself how the medical personnel who protect themselves the most are also those who complain the most of being exhausted. Those who give themselves, however, also recharge themselves at the same time. There's a phrase of Lou Andreas Salomé, one of the first women to follow in

Freud's footsteps in the practice of psychoanalysis: "It is in giving oneself that one possesses oneself completely." In all her exchanges with the master of psychoanalysis, which are so subtle and full of intelligence, she never ceased to preach the lesson that love, far from being a reservoir that begins to drain with use, refills the more it overflows.

THOSE, like myself, who accompany the dying know just how much we receive as a gift simply by accepting the commitment to embark on this ultimate experience in a human relationship that is proffered to us by the dying patient, sometimes even unconsciously. The gamble of this ultimate relationship seems to reside in the attempt to reveal oneself as one really is, or, to use Michel de M'Uzan's expression, to "give birth to oneself in the world before leaving it."*

THE INTENSITY of this surge of emotion in some people in the prelude to death seems to be proportional to their sense of urgency. The person who feels death coming has no more time to lose. He or she will engage with full force, and needs to feel this being reciprocated.

I TRY TO MAKE my doubting colleague understand how indispensable the presence of another human

---

*Michel de M'Uzan, "The Work of Death," in *From Art to Death* (Paris: Gallimard, 1977), pp. 182–99.

being is. There has to be someone else to share this ultimate experience of connection—someone emotionally open, who will not shy away; someone who can remain open to these emotional demands without feeling threatened. This is precisely what those around the dying often find hard to bear, and if they run away so often, it's because they don't understand the meaning of this sudden vitality and they're afraid it can drag them into death, as well.

I REMEMBER a woman of about fifty who spent several weeks begging for euthanasia, then suddenly reversed herself and wanted to spend whatever time was left to her deepening her relationship with her family. In the face of this unexpected request, the family, which had been preparing for weeks for the death of their relative, was caught completely off guard. Confronted with her relatives' inability to respond to her intense need for communication, she turned to members of the unit and voluntary workers and then me. Her emotional need was as intense as it was urgent. What she required was to be able to find a welcoming ear for her sudden outpouring of deep affection for her family, which she had never allowed herself to express before. This need to give voice to her generosity was strong enough to enable her to forgive them for being unable, or not knowing how, to respond to her urge for emotional connection.

SUCH an engagement of self is possible only because it is by definition limited in duration.

The time in question is very precise: the last moments of life, hours, days, perhaps weeks at most. The freedom that flows from this very temporariness allows one to step into the "mortal orbit of the dying" without too much empathetic distress but with a real openness—because it is a fact that at this advanced stage, any emotional retreat is fatal.

I UNDERSTAND the astonishment of this man, a psychoanalyst, who says he has never even shaken hands with a patient. Accompanying the dying requires a kind of relationship that certainly has no roots in classical psychoanalysis. Nonetheless, I remain convinced that one can remain an analyst—which is to say, alert to the unconscious and to the psychic dynamic at work in these last moments of life—and still accomplish this task of initiation, of giving oneself totally to the sharing of this last journey.

◇

THIS morning, Danièle was visited by a neurologist. She asked him questions, the most delicate of which was certainly "Would her illness go into remission?" He told her that he didn't know.

"I can't tell what effect his words had on me," she writes when I go and sit down beside her and ask how she is. "I'll have to wait and see. This isn't the story I tell myself: Mine finishes better. Will I change stories, or will I keep mine? The best should be not to have one at all, but until that point, I'm protected by my campaign to get better. I will keep note of my dreams: They know more than I do!"

This lucidity and subtlety always touch me to the core.

❖

DANIÈLE has had a dream.

"I'm in the country. There are a lot of people. Suddenly, we're in a field of land mines. Some people step on the mines, others stand still to avoid stepping on them, and I say to myself, Doing nothing so as to avoid dying is not a life! So I go forward, aware of the risk (if you want to live, you have to accept the risk of death)."

Then she adds: "Paralysis and immobility are not living! If you want to escape, you have to take a big chance."

"What chance, Danièle?"

"I'll tell you what I've learned by experience: The people who are afraid are the ones who refuse death."

What is she trying to tell me? She seems so far from realizing how imminent death is for her.

I take my own risk and ask, "And you—are you afraid of death?"

The reply is as simple as it is enigmatic.

"No, I'm not afraid. I think that's where I'll meet *the* answer to *the* question."

Danièle has stopped writing. I sense that she's trying to look at me. This is not easy, because she cannot turn her head. So I move into her line of vision.

"It's what I feel myself, and you couldn't say it better," I tell her, full of gratitude for so much intelligence.

❖

LOUIS is stretched out fully dressed on the big double bed in his apartment overlooking the Seine, which he loves so much. I note, as always, how elegantly he is turned out, but also how tired and weak he looks, and that he has a big gash on his forehead. Several days ago, he canceled our rendezvous at the Promenade de Venus. He had tripped and fallen in front of his fireplace, hitting his head badly. His legs had suddenly gone from under him. Since then, he hasn't dared to go out alone.

SITTING on the edge of the mattress, I find myself at his bedside for the first time. That's when I realize that Louis is truly ill. For as long as we met at the bistro, the disease was kept at a respectful distance. We spoke about it, yes, but as if we were discussing a distant lover. Now the lover is right here, as we can feel, and we speak in almost hushed tones, as if afraid to rouse her.

Louis feels his strength ebbing away; he's getting thinner and thinner, and he is almost blind in his left eye. These are the ravages of AIDS.

"I don't think I've got very much longer," he says, patting the back of my hand gently, as if to counteract the effect of his words. Then, after a long sigh, he says, "Sometimes I want to die." It obviously relieves him to be able to say this, but then, as if he felt he didn't have the right to want to die, he goes on: "Thanks to God, I'm still alive, and I hope I can get through this summer as well as possible, for Lila's sake. I don't want to spoil her vacation."

THE APARTMENT is quiet. There's something in Louis's eyes that makes me talk to him, some kind of readiness. It seems like the right moment.

"Louis, are there things you'd like to talk to me about now, to do with what you just said, about your death being close?"

I have learned not to let slip this moment, when death is still some way away, when it is possible to talk lucidly and relatively calmly with someone about how he or she wants to die, and to be accompanied. Many sick people with whom I've been able to broach these questions soon enough have been comforted by being able to put words to their wants: having this person or that at one's side; not having emergency resuscitation or intravenous feeding, or any other kind of tubal intervention; being surrounded by calm and silence, or alternatively by music; being assured that one's body will be tended and one will be clean and presentable.

YES, NOW's the moment. Louis thanks me for thinking of it. He doesn't want to die in a hospital; above all, he doesn't want any emergency lifesaving measures. He wants to die at home, surrounded by his books, in the atmosphere he knows and loves, with his beloved Lila at his side. But on the other hand, he doesn't want to be a burden on her, or to make his last moments a trial for everyone else. He wants me to know that if things become too difficult, he will agree to go to the Hospital of Good Help, and the unit that he knows to be humane, where he already goes regularly as an outpatient.

So LOUIS makes me the repository of his wishes. For the moment, he cannot make them known to those around him. He knows they are still full of hope. They wouldn't want to hear any talk of his death yet. And he's protecting them. He knows that when the day comes, I will always be able to transmit what he told me, if he is unable to do it himself.

"What I'm most afraid of is losing my mind." For the first time, I see naked anguish in his eyes. What can I do but receive his anguish and open it up to the heavens? Faced with other people's pain, I have learned to accept it and make an offering of it. My inspiration is a very ancient Tibetan exercise in compassion: *Tonglen* (the Tibetan word that means "to give and to receive") consists of accepting another's suffering and distress, and making an offering in return for all the confidence and serenity one can muster. This simple sharing of someone else's suffering means being with him or her, not leaving that person alone.

WHAT else do I have to offer up to this look of such distress except my own confidence? I cannot reassure him with mere words, because it is possible that what he fears most may indeed happen. All I can do is to support with all my heart that part of him that will stand and face his fate, come what may. Louis has closed his eyes and folded his hands on his chest, a gesture he often makes when he is collecting his thoughts. He knows how to find the strength he needs inside himself.

I HAVE to go now. Even though he has promised himself to last through the summer, I cannot help feeling, as I hug him, the pain of never seeing him again. Each of our meetings could also be the last. Even if this is a truism for all of us, at any moment, it doesn't mean that it is easy to say good-bye to someone you are not sure you will ever see again.

My throat is tight as I hold his frail body against my heart.

As he hugs me close in turn, he says, "You know, Marie, there's nothing to understand. There's no point in trying to understand; it's all a mystery. You just have to live the mystery."

As I go down the stairs, I jot this sentence into the little beige leather notepad that Louis gave me some months ago so I could keep a record of thoughts that come to me. I scribble it down as if it were a key. It links itself with my innermost preoccupation: Is there any meaning in suffering?

❖

ON MY WAY HOME, I think over all the patients who have articulated to me their sense of revolt: "Why? Why me?" The search for the root cause of illness. The feeling of injustice. I think about the young girl I saw a few days ago at the hospital, in despair, undone. She had slept twice with a boy she met at a party, and then when she went to give blood—as she does every year—they found she was HIV-positive. Twenty-three years old! Why her?

I REMEMBER a recent conversation with the priest of the parish next to ours. This man is particularly aware of the AIDS epidemic. He said, "If each of us had to reap the fruit of our acts, I would have been in prison long since, and I would have AIDS. Why are some people affected, why do others go free? It's time we stopped searching for the cause of suffering. We're in the vale of tears, and we know that this life is only the anteroom of the true life to come."

WE SHOULD stop asking ourselves "Why?" As Louis says, there is nothing there to understand. But looking at terminal suffering and posing the question "For what?" seems to be the only way to give meaning to it. For what? Into which paths, toward which experience of life, which awareness does my illness or my suffering lead me? Can I turn it into a source of light and love? Louis told me one day that his illness had brought him to the essence of things. He had felt himself being planed by it, to the point where his capacity for joy and humility was laid bare. To the point where all excess of vanity, greed, and ridiculous pretension was cut away to expose the precariousness of life, and the impermanence of all things. His life became a slow letting go, which he described as being both total and gentle, the way Pascal describes it in the Memorial, which he reads and rereads: "Joy, joy, joy, tears of joy." The more he feels the sickness wear him away, the more he experiences this feeling of wild, intimate joy. Who can understand it? Remembering the last lines of an essay he has just finished reading about an unknown adventurer, he says of this man what he is inhibited from saying about himself, whether out of modesty or natural discretion: "His whole being was turning to dust, yet his heart burned, broken but aflame."

❖

"I'M AWARE of all the violent feelings my body arouses in people: violent fear, violent denial, or simply violent distress."

Danièle has tapped out this little message to me. She wants me to know that she sees all the upset in those around her. But, paradoxically, her intuition of this also helps her to feel less alone. She, too, feels the same thing but she cannot act out her feelings.

Right now, Jean-Marie is with her—the man she loved, with whom she experienced both the joys of passion and the agony of separation, but who is here beside her now, because even if life parts us, the bonds of love never weaken.

To Jean-Marie, who at times cannot stop the tears that come to his eyes, she writes: "The only people I can talk to are the ones who are grieving, like you. Perhaps grief has a right to come out, since it's there; after all, we're allowed it, you and I. My hands ache to hold yours; my lips ache to speak words to you, to be able to give you a normal smile."

❖

"MEDICAL science is abandoning me again; the only thing left is faith" is how Danièle begins our conversation today. She seems to understand increasingly that the medical prognosis is not good.

Danièle has had no religious education. She

comes from a family of nonobservant Polish Jews, and she considers herself an atheist.

Her first contact with some form of spirituality came eight years ago, more or less by chance, from reading Krishnamurti. Since then, every time she has faced a trial, she has passages of his writings read to her and undoubtedly draws strength from them.

She says she particularly appreciates his summons to a quest for unity within oneself and the unity among self, others, and the natural world. She approves of his warnings against any submission to this or that fashionable guru or sect.

Nothing, she says, is more foreign to her than prayer. "If I admit that there's a Creator behind creation, I believe he has a lot better things to do than listen to our babblings."

Nonetheless, she has made her first discovery of a kind of meditation by surrendering herself to the living silence and beauty of nature.

God? She doesn't believe in Him. "I don't believe in a God of justice, or a God of love. It's too human to be possible. What a lack of imagination! But nor do I believe that we can just be reduced to some bundle of atoms. Whatever tells us that there's something beyond matter—call it soul, or spirit, or consciousness, whatever you prefer—I believe in the immortality of *that*. Reincarnation or arriving at an entirely new plane of being—it's discovery by death!"

This is the first time Danièle has been so open about her spiritual concerns. The energy she gives to writing this out bears witness to the importance of this act for her—it is as if she were giving us her spiritual testament.

"If I've always had the hope that there's a place beyond death, I think it's naïve to imagine that it bears any resemblance to life as we know it."

She has read books that suggest a convergence between modern physics and Oriental philosophy. But she thinks there's still a long way to go before one will explain the other. And in a witty conclusion, she writes, "Perhaps it's not such a bad thing that the act of faith is not replaced by the act of reason."

◇

THE APPROACH of death sometimes rekindles old fears and insecurities. It's understandable that as one loses one's defenses and protective mechanisms, one becomes extremely vulnerable. Sometimes pains and terrors come surging back from earliest childhood. Doesn't every human being search for the protection and security that have been lacking?

IN ROOM 775, Christine is going through moments of terror like these, which are as uncontrollable as they are unforeseeable. This young woman, who's barely thirty years old and is dying of a uterine cancer that has spread, is somehow seized with panic. She sees her room filled with a mass of serpents writhing on her bed. She jumps up, screaming. This scene has already taken place more than once. The team is in disarray; the patients in the neighboring rooms are terrified. What's going on?

Despite the fact Christine is receiving treatment specially tailored for this kind of hallucination, the terrors keep coming, though they subside after the initial moments. The rest of the time, she is fairly serene; indeed, I would describe her as showing surprising maturity in her way of living this last phase of her life, a maturity in striking contrast to her attacks of a child's panic. She talks openly about her death and is much taken up with what will happen to her fiancé, telling him repeatedly that she wants him to make a new life with another woman as soon as he can.

THIS morning, when I arrive in the unit, I see Christine, haggard, in the middle of the hall, screaming at the top of her lungs and being restrained with considerably difficulty by Dr. Clement and Simone, who each have hold of one arm and are trying to stop her from running away. Because that's what she's trying to do.

Of course I lend a hand. Christine is shouting that the serpents are after her and is begging for protection. Without really thinking I take her in my arms. She's so light that I have no difficulty in carrying her into the little sitting room nearby. There, I collapse on the settee, holding her tightly to me, and begin to rock her gently as I sing her name. After assuring himself that I don't need him, Dr. Clement goes out and closes the door, because Christine is still making quite a lot of noise, though she's no longer trying to get away. I feel she's comfortable about sitting here on my knee; she even feels safe with my arms round her to protect her from this invisible danger.

While her cries continue, I just rock her against me, making a little song of her name, over and over again.

143

She's quieted down now but is convulsed with sobs, her head pressed into my neck like a child. Then, in a voice that is suddenly a little girl's, choked with tears, she tells me about her childhood terrors. Her mother collected live snakes in a big glass jar and let them out whenever Christine misbehaved. It's hard for me to believe such cruelty, hard to believe any mother could do something so mad. And it's really not important whether this is a fantasy or reality. These fears are an integral part of Christine's childhood. My task is simply to allow her to know that there are other places where one can feel safe. She, too, has a safe place. Right now, for the moment, it's here in my arms, and in another moment, it will be somewhere else. What better thing could I do than allow her to live this moment of feeling completely secure?

Her tears have stopped now. The young woman is playing with the butterfly made of blue beads strung by some children with leukemia. I wear it on the lapel of my white coat, its head always touching my shoulder. I stroke her long blond hair, which reaches to the middle of her back.

"I'll give it to you if you like," I say. "Butterflies don't get caught by snakes; it'll protect you." My butterfly will be a transitional object. This is what the English psychiatrist Winnicott calls the object the child can keep hold of, which allows him or her to bear the absence of the mother, insofar as the object can be invested with her qualities.

Now that Christine is calm again and ready to be taken back to her room, I tell her that the butterfly is the symbol of the soul, the very essence of humanity—which escapes the laws of biology—what I believe to be man's share of eternity. Christine has no trouble with this idea: she believes that her soul is immortal, too.

◇

IN THE NEXT room, there's a man about sixty, groaning. Curled up in a fetal position, facing the window, he's in pain.

Ever since he arrived last night, he's been complaining of sharp pains in his back. Reading the nurse's report from the night, I see that his morphine has been increased a little. But the doctor is puzzled. The man has lung cancer, and even if this has metastasized into the bones, it would in no way explain what he describes as intense pelvic spasms of pain, as if he's in labor.

The room is in almost total darkness. The shades have remained down, at the request of the patient. Everything in his posture declares that he wants to fold himself away, separate himself from the external world. It's as if he's curled himself up in order to fit into an imaginary shell.

I have come in on tiptoe and moved around the bed. Has he heard me? Apparently yes, because he half-opens his eyes. I smile at him. He makes a move as if to give me his hand, which I take as an invitation to stay. I move closer, and, laying my hand very gently on his hip, I ask if he can make room for me on the bed without having to change position.

"I'll sit here in this little hollow," I say as I let myself down onto the bed. "That way, you can curl up around me." And indeed, he rolls his body a little closer against me. When I ask him where exactly he feels pain, he points to the whole lumbar region.

From my sitting position, I'm able to massage the painful area very gently and cradle him a little.

He seems to appreciate it, and he sighs with relief. "That feels good. You know, I feel as if I'm in childbirth."

He barely has time to say this before being seized by a fit of violent sobbing. I don't move, and I don't say a word. It is a fact familiar to me from frequent observation that the simple reality of being touched with gentle respect can sometimes unleash the most powerful emotional reactions. For even the skin itself possesses a memory, and a simple touch, if it feels *good* and *reaffirming*, can trigger the reexperiencing of the most deep-rooted deprivation and distress.

"What are you feeling?"

"As I said that to you, I thought of my mother, and it hurt me a lot. I was an unwanted child, and my mother tried everything she could to get rid of me in the first months of her pregnancy. She never loved me, and I think I'm going to die knowing that."

How can one die in the knowledge of never having been welcomed into life? This elderly man has assumed a fetal position as a sign to us of his distress: I cannot let myself go into the arms of death without ever having known in my life the feeling of going into my mother's arms.

◇

ANGUISH, despair, pain—all must be able to declare themselves, even cry out sometimes. In hospitals, all too often there's a tendency to suppress any expression of emotion around a dying patient. Every possible tranquilizer is used to ensure that the dying person plays dead. He or she absolutely must be kept calm and quiet. There is an enveloping silence, if not an outright lie, that protects the living against the sound of the voice that threatens to break through this wall, crying, "I'm afraid. I'm going to die. I'm in agony."

This is the voice that is suffocated all too often. What can one say, what can one do in the face of this appeal? It is denied because no one can endure the knowledge of being useless. Who asks us to *do* anything? Does the person who's dying expect us to halt death? Or is the person who's dying actually begging us for permission to give voice to pain and fear and the sound of a last cry?

THE FRIENDS I'm having dinner with tonight, who are mostly members of the Paris intelligentsia, have a very false idea of palliative care. What they see in it is a velvet-handed attempt to conceal what is awkward and sordid in death. One of them even uses the expression "dying in luxury." They talk about the denial of suffering, someone uses the etymology of the verb *to palliate* (*pallium* is the Latin word for coat) to support the argument about concealment. I fight hard to try to undo this false image. No, we do not clamp a lid on people's pain, as if we refuse to see or hear it, and if we envelop it, it's in a mantle of warmth and tenderness, to make it just that little bit easier to bear. I quote the recently discovered blessing from the Koran: "May you be wrapped in tenderness, you my brother, as if in a cloak."

And I ask the question: "If you put a coat around the shoulders of someone who's suffering, does that deny his pain?"

I also mention one of our patients, a woman who has converted to Buddhism, who requested when she first arrived in the unit that she not be given any painkillers. She had her own way of manufacturing endorphins by chanting "OM." I do not know of many places that would have respected her wish and accepted, as we did, day after day of the mournful droning of this mantra. Some of the nurses who were accompanying her also joined in, intoning the sacred vowels "AOUM."

❖

DANIÈLE'S sister Gisèle has left again for Cuba. This separation is as bad as a bereavement for the twins. Danièle is struck down. She has a fever, and she huddles under the bedclothes. She cries a lot and scarcely writes at all.

This afternoon, we listened to Fauré's Requiem, about which she had once said, "If there's one piece of music that leads you to God, it's this."

I cradled her the whole time; she was like a miserable little girl.

❖

THE FEVER has broken. Danièle's back at her computer. What would her life be like if she didn't have this means of communicating with us? She is beginning to worry about her group of friends, all of whom are beginning to show signs of the stress of this constant companionship. It's true that the obligation to maintain a permanent vigil is a heavy one to incur, now that Gisèle is no longer there. She's afraid of being a burden on those around her.

"One exceeds one's bounds without being aware of it, and relations start to deteriorate," she warns. "You are my life support: So go out and live!"

◆

IN THE ROOM next door, an old lady of ninety-two is dying—serenely.

Taking my hands, she says, "My child, life is generous to those who seize it with both hands. Don't be afraid of anything. Live! Live, whatever presents itself to you, because everything is a gift from God!"

There's so much fire and passion in this last message. I've stopped in this room for only a moment. I'm almost unknown to her, and yet this dying old lady gives me her last word on living.

I go out of the room full of life and love. It feels as if the old lady has fanned my own life's flame with her last breaths. Such an unanticipated gift.

◆

DANIÈLE'S friends have found a young helper to take care of her at night. He's young, very handsome, Oriental. Contact is established right away. He knows how to talk to Danièle; best of all, he's *there*, calm and reassuring. His knowledge of Chinese medicine, with its concept of vital energy, allows him to take care of Danièle in a totally new way. He invites her to move in her spirit. Her muscles can no longer respond, but she can feel a way toward him; she can stretch out to him with every atom of her being, every particle of her soul. It's a new and creative way of thought that has everything it takes to revive our patient. In no time at all, she has fallen in love with this beautiful man and is filled with the joy of a heart that's alive again.

Most extraordinary of all, the doctors find evidence of improvement in her muscles. Danièle is thrilled.

"I can turn my hand palm-up! It's pathetic and extraordinary at the same time. I'm exerting all my strength, and all my hopes. Maybe the course of history can reverse itself; at least I want to believe it can. Everyone here is so enthusiastic. That increases my own hope. Nobody's talking about a miracle, but all the attention they're giving me is its own encouragement. No long discussions! All anyone says with a big grin is, 'Show me' when this stupid thing twitches (every time it does, it makes me think of some unlucky fish out of water, giving its last hiccup on the sand)." What a sense of humor!

IT'S TRUE that the whole team is fascinated by signs of progress, which seem to call into question the diagnosis of ALS. If Danièle starts to recover, would we not have to send her on to a different unit for rehabilitative medicine? It's a real question.

◇

MONTREAL. The conference on "Healing Beyond Suffering or Death" is coming to an end. The Dalai

Lama has come to preside over the last full session. I am sitting in the first row with Luc Bessette. The visionary organizer of this huge conference has been kind enough to invite me to do this. More than fifteen hundred people have come for two days to discuss issues raised by illness and death. It is the first time an international scientific congress has given major time to Oriental traditions and techniques of meditation.

Silence falls in the huge hall as the Dalai Lama arrives on the platform. A young boy, very frail, head shaved and the skin almost translucent, goes up the steps to the side. It's clear that we're looking at a sick child, though he holds himself absolutely erect. A woman leads him in front of the Dalai Lama, says a few words, and the holy man bends down toward the child. The two shaved heads, one tanned and brown, the other almost transparently white, are now touching forehead to forehead. There is something profoundly moving in this encounter between the elderly sage and the sick child. A man at the microphone explains that the child has leukemia and his life is in danger because all the treatments have failed. The boy's greatest wish was to have the chance someday to meet the Dalai Lama. That wish has now been granted.

The old monk seats the child to his right at the conference table and the last speakers at the conference succeed one another at the microphone. Finally, it is time for questions from the floor. Luc Bessette turns to the child and asks, "Can you tell us what you most need at this point in your illness? And can you tell us what death means for you?"

The child takes the microphone and, with an unshakable inner authority, answers in a voice that is as calm as it is amazingly poised: "What I need is for people to treat me as if I weren't ill. For them to laugh and have fun with me and just be natural. I know I'm only here for a limited time, to learn something. When I've learned what I've been born to learn, I'll leave. But in my head, I cannot imagine life stopping."

WHICH is how fifteen hundred educated people this afternoon were given the most beautiful lesson in wisdom and simplicity. Golden words in the mouth of a child condemned by medical science. A great rustle went through the hall; then there was absolute silence. Lots of people had tears in their eyes. The old monk stood up and bowed to the child, as he would have done to a master. He laid a white scarf over the boy's shoulders and blessed him. The hall erupted in applause, which went on and on. It was the audience's only way to articulate its emotions.

◇

AFTER Montreal, I want to go and spend a few days at the home for AIDS patients in Quebec. It's a unique institution, unlike anything we have in France, because the public authorities have always been opposed to the creation of special places for people infected with the virus. The arguments are always the same: no sanAIDtoriums (the word was coined by the right-wing leader, Mr. Le Pen), no exclusionary institutions. Out of a wish to avoid any segregation, all projected homes like the ones that have come into existence in Canada have been quashed until very recently—even though they could be places of rare humanity. But things are beginning to move. A palliative care home for people with terminal AIDS is already advancing beyond the planning stage in Gardanne, which is in Provence. The director of the project has contacted me with an invitation to help with the training of the future team. It's with this in mind that I'm visiting the Marc-Simon House today.

JOCELYNE, the nun who runs the home, has come to meet me at the bus bringing me from Montreal. I've already met her several times before, and her radiant goodness has made a deep impression on me. She has nothing of the narrow dogmatism or bigoted rigidity that can afflict some in the religious life. She's simply a woman who is sensitive to the suffering of others, as discreet as she is good. And the residents of Marc-Simon know it: They love her.

"THEY'RE so happy you're coming," she says. And I'm aware of the special way she has of opening doors for me. Her car draws up outside an ordinary little building, a family house surrounded by a small garden. We've arrived.

Jocelyne points out the elevator, a new addition, which allows the resident patients to stay until the very end. The house has ten bedrooms and is divided into two floors. On the ground floor, there's a big kitchen connecting with the dining room, which is the most used place in the house. I meet Lise, a welcoming young woman who's in charge of the cooking. She's busy making a chocolate cake, and the house is filled with delicious smells. She obviously loves her work. The sitting room opens onto the garden. I say hello to a tall boy who's deep in an armchair, with a rug over his legs. He looks very frail, but his face has the calm and openness that so touches me in these dying young people. An older man, who could be his father, is talking to him quietly. The tenderness in the exchange is self-evident. Next door is the smoking room, where two boys who are emaciated but can still move without help are drawing on their cigarettes and talking in such strong Quebec accents that I cannot understand a word. It will take some days for my ear to adapt to this form of French. Jocelyne takes me on a tour of the house, introducing me to this one and that. I'm able to meet the residents—as they call the patients here—the families, and the volunteers, who follow each other in shifts, offering a little of their time and their attention.

I am struck by how much of a family atmosphere the house has. There's not a hint of a hospital ambience. You finally forget about the illness altogether. This impression is reinforced at lunchtime. The residents come downstairs one by one and sit around the table. A man arrives in a wheelchair, barely able to sit upright. Yet he insists on coming to the table. He looks like a youthful old man. He hardly touches the few spoonfuls of puree that Lise puts on his plate. It doesn't matter; what's important is being here to share the moment with the others. He follows the conversation with huge, attentive eyes. Lise has just brought in a steaming soup tureen. One of the residents, who has just finished his second year here and is obviously the one who's been there longest, points out to me how much the tureen symbolizes everything they love about this house, the conviviality and human warmth.

They ask me to tell them about what I did in Montreal. I talk about the last session of the conference and the child with leukemia. The man in the wheelchair is watching me intensely. "The child's right." He sighs. I notice that Lise has taken account of everyone's individual tastes and preferences. Each day, she prepares endless tiny dishes, carefully garnished, conscious of how important it is that they look appealing, because many of the residents cannot really eat any longer, but they continue to come to the table, as if it were enough to feed the eyes and the heart. Conversation flows naturally, sometimes serious, sometimes lighthearted, among these men who are living out their final days. There are some silences, but they're not heavy; they just feel necessary. No one tries to fill them with clumsy remarks.

THIS is a place where life is truly being lived, moment by moment, as it should be.

I GET UP FROM the table, full of admiration. In the pause that follows, when everyone seems to go off for a nap, I chat with Lise while she clears the plates. She says she sees miracles here every day. The residents support one another, and this solidarity is an inspiration. She is still recovering from the death of a man named Jean the week before, and she wants to talk to me about it. We sit down again at the table with a cup of coffee, now that the dining room is empty, and she tells me:

"Jean was a dancer. When he got here, he had enormous KS lesions which had invaded his legs and lower body. It was horrible to see such putrefaction. And he was in such pain. Morphine did help a bit, of course, but he made immense efforts to come to meals. Once he got there, he told us stories and made us laugh. He had the most extraordinary moral strength. I know for sure that he gave courage to everyone else. He used to say, 'Come on, guys, our bodies have gone to hell, but our spirits are free.' He was full of joie de vivre."

As I listen, I think about Patrick and Louis and so many others who teach us the basics.

"Just before he died, Jean sent for his friend. He asked him to hold his hands and dance with him. He wanted to remain a dancer to the very end. Jean lifted himself a little and with his friend's help began with all his heart to make his arms dance, while his friend wept uncontrollably. 'Dance, dance,' he kept saying as their linked arms swayed from left to right. Then Jean smiled a magnificent, transcendent smile and collapsed back onto the pillow. He had died in his dance.

"There were several residents there in the room, who will all die soon themselves. They said that Jean's death had banished their fears about the actual moment of death. They know that if there's enough love and tenderness around them, things will go the way they should go, quite simply, perhaps even the way that, deep down, they want them to happen. But they say this shyly, as if such convictions should not be shouted from the rooftops.

"These are the powerful moments that give us the strength to go on working here. Because you know, it's hard, very hard, and it uses you up. To watch them fade and get weak, and leave us. Sometimes you get a kind of vertigo from the endless passing column of young people wasting away into death. It will never end. When I reach the end of my tether, when I doubt that there's any point to what I'm doing, I go and open the consolation box, where we keep the letters from the residents' families thanking us for what we've done, and pieces of paper with beautiful quotations that lift our hearts and spirits."

❖

He wanted it so much. And so Louis has made it through the summer. But coming back to an empty and deserted Paris, the way it can be in August, is miserable. Louis is barely able to get out of bed anymore, as the least physical exertion is completely exhausting. Lila has gone back to work. So he spends most of the day alone, stretched out on his big bed, with a book in his hands which he sometimes lets slip, because he falls asleep at unexpected moments.

What he most feared has now happened. Louis is losing his sense of things. His speech is becoming confused. He can no longer keep his bearings. As soon as I get back, I hurry to see him. Lila opens the door to me, and from her face I can tell things are bad. She comes straight into my arms, and she's in tears. The doctor is apparently talking about premature senility. It's the irreversibility of the diagnosis that is so distressing.

"You see, he forgets everything; everything's a muddle, and he was always so brilliant and so subtle. The thought that we can never communicate again is agony."

The doctor has mentioned palliative care, and Lila understands that Louis has begun the last stage of his life. So she has to grieve twice over—preparing for Louis's death and mourning the loss of an intellectual relationship full of nuances.

"Lila dear."

I hold my arms tightly around this young woman and her sorrow. I, too, feel devastated. How can I help?

LOUIS greets me with obvious emotion. His whole body is trembling and a flood of incomprehensible words is trying to tell me something. But no matter how I listen and seize a word here and there that might form a path, I struggle in vain to understand. So I sit next to him, and he huddles against me. He seems to need gentle, silent contact. He likes it when I softly lay my hands on his sick eyes and on all the places on his body that hurt him—his legs, his clenched solar plexus. He likes the feeling of being touched with physical respect; it makes him feel he's still a living human being. He once described this kind of attention that my hands are giving him as "caressing the soul." Contact with my patients, who are so withdrawn into the interior suffering of their ruined bodies, has taught me to develop a tactile approach to them, a form of touch that helps them to feel complete and alive. What is needed is to envelop the aching skin of a dying body with a second, more subtle, more ethereal skin, a psychic, spiritual one.

Sometimes there is no substitute for the touch of a hand. It embodies the sense of true meeting. As I hold Louis's face in my hands and take in all its lostness as his features soften and his skin warms to my touch, the contact between us is profound. Nothing is said, but we are together.

When I see nurses keeping their arms straight and stiff while they're taking care of patients, I often tell them that if they curve their arms and make a cradle of them, their movements will be imbued with delicacy and tenderness. The heart's warmth will be awakened and will radiate outward into the hands.

This contact of essence to essence is something that must be risked, essayed, lived. This is what I want to tell Lila as I come out of the bedroom. Yes, Louis's universe has shrunk. His body is almost about to disappear. His mind is regressing. But his heart and soul are both intact. Is it not true to say that there is a new and different distribution of vital energy at the end of life? As physical and intellectual powers diminish, is there not a corresponding gain in emotional and psychic capacity? Is it not precisely because the world of the person who is dying is shrinking, because their days are numbered, that last conversations, the words it is still possible to exchange, shared glances, the feeling of skin on skin, become irreplaceable?

WHERE is Louis to be encountered anymore if not in the rustle of emotions? What meaning can his life have now that he is no longer able to read or express a coherent thought? Some people say that a life that no longer permits one to be true to oneself is hardly worth living. They dwell on the loss of dignity. What they forget is the unsuspected resources that still lie unawakened in the depths of one's being, the treasure one has never mined because one has had others to draw on—an entire interior life, intimate, emotional, spiritual. There is much to learn, in someone's dying, from these neglected registers of our deepest selves. And perhaps there is much we can teach when we ourselves die.

I am very conscious of how much I am given and how much I keep learning from those who can no longer do anything except be there—from those who can offer only their smile or their wide-open gaze, or their dignity in allowing themselves to be cared for. They have taught me simplicity, and humanity.

◇

I AM SITTING in the little gray salon next to François Mitterrand's bedroom in the Elysée Palace. The president, whom I called yesterday, asked me to come and see him. He has just left the hospital. Like the world in general, I know from the newspapers that he has had an operation for cancer. "I'm soon going to need your palliative care," is what he said to me.

The room is groaning with books, pictures, pieces of sculpture—presents given to the president— which he keeps here under the gaze of these dark walls until he can send them to the Nièvre Museum, to which he consigns them all. It's Saturday afternoon, silent, gloomy, and cold.

A DOOR opens. The footman announces that the president will receive me. I'm ushered into the beautiful bedroom with its pale paneling and elegant proportions. The room is agreeably welcoming and calm, in contrast to the antechamber. The president is in bed. His customary aura of dignity seems to have followed him even into this intimate place. It derives, as I know, not just from his position but from his personality. There is something in this man as he lies there that commands respect even as it suggests his utterly accessible humanity. His face looks drawn, but he seems very calm. I go over and sit on his bed, the way I often do in the hospital. I have always had a simple and straightforward relationship with this man, who now greets me like a friend and tells me with absolute directness what's happening to him.

"THE PROCESS has begun. The illness is fatal, I know. . . ." His voice is calm; he is looking directly into my eyes. "I'm not afraid of death, but I love life. It always comes too soon." Then we talk about time, and the amount he has left to live. Nobody can give him a prognostication about this. The will to live often wins out over medical opinion. I've seen it often myself.

"You mustn't start dying before death comes," I say. We both know that one can be clear-minded about the approach of death and yet continue to have all sorts of plans. It's a matter of staying absolutely alive until the end.

The president wonders if believers face death with greater serenity. Is there a connection between faith and peace of mind? Our conversations about death have often turned toward the mystical. Could it be otherwise? Can one talk about the eternal mystery that is death without evoking our connection to the invisible, given everything we cannot explain, but only intuit? The president, who describes himself as agnostic, says this doesn't stop him from having a religious belief—that he is linked to some dimension beyond himself. The experience is both sensorial and intimate, which, he says, is more of an argument for the existence of God than any article of faith provides.

"One can be a nonbeliever and yet serene in the face of death; one can prepare for it as for a journey into the unknown. After all, the unknown is simply another form of the beyond," he posits.

I tell him about a woman who met her death with absolute serenity recently, and who had said to me, "I'm not a believer, but I am curious to know what's coming next." Is this not a form of faith, this confidence in the unfolding of things? Belief in something after death is not much help if it is not rooted in the experience of a deep inner trust. I have known two priests who were each in absolute torment on their deathbeds, unable to pray or to let themselves go.

"It's not faith, but the texture of a life lived that allows one to give oneself into the arms of death," I say.

We talk quietly about dying. It is such a gift to share a moment's intimacy with a man who has so little time left—so little time for himself, so little privacy, even though he has always fought to preserve that for himself.

The president starts talking about his visit to the palliative care unit. "What a wonderful experience!" The calm of the patients he met is still vivid in his mind. He says he hopes with all his heart that when the time comes, he will be able to retain this self-mastery to the end. "I know I'll need you. You don't bring peace to your patients just by talking to them—

you do it by being there. You allow people to let themselves go."

His confidence is touching. Of course it would be a privilege to accompany him through his last moments. He knows I feel that.

I don't know how we come around to talking about the inner strength that comes to us when times are worst. Can one rely on oneself? He and I have often talked about meditation and prayer—regathering one's troubled spirits into one's innermost self, creating silence, listening to the breath of life as it courses through one. Prayer has nothing to do with the perpetual droning of words, nor with requests for the impossible. In the phrase of the monk Seraphim of Savov, it is "being part of a presence that envelops both body and soul" or being in contact with the community of all who pray.

"When you pray, you rise to meet in the air those who are praying at that very hour and whom you may not meet save in prayer." The sentence is Kahlil Gibran's.

"SO YOU BELIEVE in the communion of saints?" The president says he is receptive to the idea that one cannot rely on one's own inner strength alone, and that one needs prayers, the invisible communion with others as they set their thoughts to something higher. I have often talked to him about the prayer group I belong to with friends; we dedicate some of our time and our thoughts to this spiritual communion in a form of solidarity. It is a beautiful idea to believe that at any moment on earth, thousands of people are praying, that one can link oneself to this in thought, and that one can yearn with all one's heart and soul for this shared energy to be of help to someone who is enduring loneliness or suffering.

❖

DANIÈLE'S condition has suddenly worsened. She is having difficulty breathing. Her muscular "recovery" has ceased. What is left to her is her love for the young helper, which illuminates every moment of her life.

This morning, she's so exhausted that she just writes one sentence: "Happiness comes unannounced even on the wings of illness."

Then she drops off to sleep. Is she trying to tell me that this happiness is enough for her? That everything is fine like this? She seems worn-out but serene.

Yesterday, we celebrated her birthday. Christiane and Jean-Marie, her closest friends, were there. They, too, have been falling in love with each other at Danièle's bedside, and she's deeply touched by it. Life is certainly full of surprises. It has brought this young woman, stripped of all resources and on the verge of dying, the chance both to live love and to feel it.

After her birthday party, all she wrote was, "I am one of those guests who never know when to leave."

❖

DANIÈLE died this morning. She simply stopped breathing as she was being turned onto her side. Chantal, the nurse, was undone.

Now she's lying on her bed, dressed in embroidered red silk pajamas, and there are flowers in her hair. The nurse's aides wanted it that way. An expression of their admiration and gratitude, no doubt, because she taught us a lot these last months. She initiated us.

❖

THE DANCE center in the Marais is one of the liveliest places I know. It's the end of the morning on a late Saturday in September, and the courtyard at the old eighteenth-century mansion is bathed in sunlight. Every kind of music pours from the wide-open windows—a riff of jazz, the insistent rhythm of a flamenco. Then, from a little farther away, a merry explosion of taps. The clientele of the Studio, the Mexican restaurant that puts its tables out in the courtyard, is made up mostly of regulars at the dance center. They come every week to work off their tensions, ease their stiff bodies, give their spirits the chance to express themselves in movement. They come to dance life.

LILA decided some months ago to take a course in jazz dance again. I'm here to learn tango. Both of us love dancing and using this alliance of body and music to help us forget, if only for a moment, the sad things in life.

We have a rendezvous after her class to have lunch and to talk about Louis.

It might seem strange that Lila would choose a public place, a restaurant, to talk about what upsets her most deeply. One of the paradoxes about such places of transit is that they often permit greater free play to the emotions. As I've often noticed at the hospital, families prefer to talk to me at the end of the corridor, as if the passing people, the noise, the surrounding bustle form a kind of protective skin, an atmosphere of sparkling distraction that offers shelter and allows people to open up their inner selves without too much risk.

"I come unglued in bistros all the time these days," she says. How could it be otherwise? I feel so warm toward this young woman, beautiful, natural, so full of life. She loves being alive, she loves to dance, and her young husband is dying. She's only thirty-five years old, and she's getting ready for widowhood. "I have to prepare for Louis's death, and I do not know how I will be able to live without him." Great silent tears roll down her cheeks, which are still pink from dancing.

"I don't know how. I need help."

"What seems hardest to you? Is it when you're with Louis, or when you're with your friends?"

LILA has come an immense distance in recent weeks. She knows Louis is going to die, she knows he wants to die at home, and she knows he doesn't want any violent medical intervention. They share the same wavelength. They've fought his illness together for seven years. Their daily struggle has served to deepen their connection profoundly, and the strength of the resulting bond is one she speaks of with a certain pride. When she talks about their love for each other, her voice fills with tears; it conveys an indescribable pain at the thought of his absence. Then, like a diver coming back up to the surface, Lila shakes her head and picks up where she broke off. I make a mental bow to the life force that is sustaining her in this terrible moment, for she is looking things squarely in the face, denying neither her vitality nor her devastation.

She knows that the road he is on is now irreversible. What matters is to accompany the man she loves, trying to share fully his current situation.

"This morning, we spent a wonderful moment together. I sang one of Igor's alleluias to him as I stroked his face."

A few months ago, a group of us who are friends spent a weekend led by Igor Reznikoff, an exceptional expert in medieval chant. Louis and Lila were there. For three days, we were afloat on a sea of harmony, absorbing the richness of pure sound in all its bare simplicity. Reznikoff, his hair standing out every which way, was dressed in sempiternal white shirt and black trousers. Perched on a little chair facing thirty apprentices, all seated on the ground, he achieved a miracle: From these thirty more or less rusty voices he coaxed a sound that was extraordinary in its purity and beauty. We were all made conscious of the realm of sonority that made the human body into an echo chamber, a sacred place of praise. Louis loved the time spent sharing this music with his friends. He always had a passion for Gregorian chant.

. . .

AND THAT was how Lila accompanied Louis, using her voice and her hands to make a little holy space in which they could continue to communicate with each other despite the ravages of his illness.

"The hardest thing for me will be having to tell my mother and sisters that Louis is going to die. They've so supported me in the hope that he was going to conquer this. It makes me feel defeated and ashamed."

Lila is putting words to the immense loneliness she feels. Everyone around her still seems to be hoping for an improvement. The questions on the phone, the encouraging words—all their ways of reassuring ring so false now.

"I can't seem to say to them that *no*, Louis is not going to come back from this, that he's in his last weeks. I wish I could tell them to look things in the face and stop behaving like ostriches," she continues, a trace of anger in her voice.

"Yes, Lila, you need people to get on the same wavelength as you; you need people who can help you see things the way they are, the way they're going to happen. So why don't you talk to them, help them to help you, tell them what you need?"

LILA has a great gift: As soon as she sees a problem clearly, she is determined to resolve it. She knew something wasn't right about what was happening around Louis, and she wanted to talk to me about it. Now she sees it more clearly. She has to cross a threshold that she has avoided until now: bringing

168

both her family and Louis's around to recognizing reality so that they can all accompany him without further lies. She knows what she has to do.

◆

AFTER this conversation, it occurs to me that Louis's state of confusion may have something to do with the lack of clarity around him and all the ambiguous messages he is receiving. I go back in my mind to Marcelle, who reemerged from her confusion as soon as she was allowed to say that she was dying and she knew that she was understood. I recall other situations in which the conversations I've had with families have also been to clarify the situation and to make it possible for people in a state of denial to cross a barrier and see things as they really are. These conversations have had almost miraculous effects on the patient.

SEVERAL months ago, I had a visit in my office at the hospital from a fellow psychoanalyst, a woman my own age, whose daughter was dying of AIDS in our unit. Valerie was twenty-three years old. Infected several years before by a young drug addict whom she was trying to save by love, she came to us in a coma, after eight months of agony. Her parents, brothers and sisters, and friends all accompanied her through those long months, and according to her mother, the experience both undid and changed them all. Accustomed as she was, by profession, to taking part in the existential crises of her analytic patients, she admitted to having been profoundly marked by the extent of the transformation in everyone who dealt with Valerie during this time. "She took us all such a long way down our life's path. She made us advance very quickly. She initiated us without even being aware of it," she said.

THIS woman had come to see me because she didn't understand why her daughter seemed unable to die. What was going on? What was she waiting for? I tell my colleagues what I know from my own experience with the dying. Coma is a strange state. We don't know very much about it, but people who come out of it say that they could hear what was being said around them and that they were aware of the emotional effect of both words and gestures. It seems that some kind of internal work goes forward deep inside the individual. It's a mysterious state, which one is inclined to respect because it may contain important processes, and one has to be sufficiently humble to respect what one cannot understand.

I do have some hypotheses. In particular, I believe that coma is a form of refuge when things become too heavy to bear but when it is still too soon to die, because emotional accounts have not yet been settled. I've often had the impression that those in a coma were giving the people around them time to prepare for the ultimate separation. Some of them are waiting for a particular visit, or a reconciliation that has not yet taken place.

I told this woman about a man who waited for three months for a visit from his fourteen-year-old daughter, whom the family would not let see him because they were afraid of the effect on her of her father's physical deterioration. The man was able to let go and die the morning after his daughter came to say good-bye. It is impossible not to interpret this coma as a long period of waiting. Others simply wait until a loved one who is painfully attached to them and keeps them bound to life finally gives them permission to die.

I said all this to Valerie's mother, who was wondering why her daughter, who had said three weeks ago, just before sinking into a coma, that she wanted to die, was still alive.

"Is there anyone in your immediate circle who is not yet ready for Valerie to die?"

She tried to think but could not come up with anyone. As far as she knew, everyone had been preparing themselves over the intense and interminable last eight months. I just said that sometimes we think we're prepared, but something inside us is still holding back the person we love. It must be terrible for a mother to watch her young daughter die. No matter how one prepares, some part of oneself must refuse and buck against it. The woman I was talking to knew it, too, for, like me, she had learned to listen to the unconscious.

THE DAY FOLLOWING this conversation, Valerie was still in her long sleep. It had been a long time since she had given any reaction either to hearing her name or to being touched. She seemed to be in a deep coma. At noon, her father and mother arrived in the company of a volunteer who had become very attached to Valerie in the preceding days. They stood in a circle around Valerie's bed. Her mother started to speak, talking to her daughter with the greatest love and emotion.

"My darling, we're here around you. We love you. Through all your life, and particularly in these last times of your illness, you've brought us so many gifts that we'll never be able to thank you for sufficiently. God bless you, now, and go on your way. We will stay here with everything precious you've left us to help us continue without you; go, go now."

At that precise moment, Valerie came out of her coma. She opened her eyes and looked at her parents. Then she made a tiny movement of the hand and said, "Ciao," almost casually, the way she always had, and her breath ceased at this last farewell. It was over.

◇

I WAS EXPECTING this. Louis has come out of his wretched state of confusion. He has found himself again.

Lila took the initiative with her family. She managed to say that Louis was nearing his end. It was good to be able to say it at last and to cry herself out. To be held by this one, and that. To lay down her heavy burden while being held tightly as others wept, too. To feel the pain spread and circulate and finally get a little lighter. Perhaps to feel a little less lonely.

Louis was saying his good-byes—a word here, a blessing there. He has recovered both speech and coherent thought. Forty-eight hours of absolute peace.

Everyone around him starts to feel more healed, clearer, more true to themselves.

"Will they hold out?" he asks me.

HIS LAST preoccupation is with the people he is leaving behind. Several months ago, he talked about his distress at having to inflict such pain on people he loves. He prayed, he said, that they would find the strength to bear the grief through which he was going to put them. His distress is just as great today. Is he aware of how much he is giving us all by the power of his goodness and his way of meeting his own death? Of how much he has changed people's deepest selves? We are all being transformed by our contact with him. Is he at all aware of this?

"Dear Louis, I don't know how to tell you how much you do to keep me focused on what is essential. Someone said the other day that you reset all our clocks to the right time! You may not even be aware of it, but you're giving each of us the strength we can lean on later, when you're gone."

Louis thanks me with a big smile. Maybe all he needed was this confirmation. He takes my hand, lifts it to his lips, and kisses it.

"I wish you both every possible happiness." The farewell is addressed not just to me but to my husband.

❖

I HAVE come here this morning, as I promised Louis I would. As I pushed open the door to the apartment, I knew he was dead. His sister came to meet me. It's impossible to say why one knows what one knows, to what invisible signals one responds. Perhaps it was a particular kind of silence. So his sister came to meet me, saying what I already knew.

"He died half an hour ago as the nurses were washing him. Lila isn't here; she'll be back at any moment. She doesn't know yet."

I go into the bedroom. Louis's eyes and mouth are open, but his face has a certain look of astonishment. His sister is upset because the nurses cannot close his eyes or mouth. She's afraid Lila will not be able to bear it. Perhaps because I've seen it done so often at the hospital, I take my courage in both hands and perform the most intimate of all gestures, which is to close another human being's eyes. It is not an easy one. I take a last look at this frozen expression, which in some way is already not him. His eyes were always bright, and he looked you straight in the heart. His eyelids are still warm, and I weep as I pull them gently downward, as if this might hurt him. I have to do it several times over, and I understand why the nurses gave up. I ask his sister to bring me some wet cotton wool. We put a compress on each eye, and we stand there, she and I, pressing on Louis's eyes to make them finally stay closed. We also rolled a towel and tied it under his chin to raise the lower jaw and help to close his mouth. These are things done by thousands of women before us when there was a death in the family.

Lila has arrived. I can hear her weeping in the hall.

◇

THERE are about twenty of them—men and women, all supporters in the fight against AIDS, all volunteers who help those afflicted. They have received permission from the board of AIDES Provence for the creation of the palliative care unit they have been campaigning for over the last two years, because they have been emotionally bankrupted by the deaths of people they have spent months and years tending as this terrible illness runs it course. Some have lost ten or twelve friends this way—for how could you not form deep bonds with people when you become witness to their personal suffering? Some of them are themselves HIV-positive. They make no secret of the fact that helping the sick gives meaning to their lives and that accompanying those ahead of them on the road to death is a form of initiation. None of that diminishes the fact that such an activity is taxing in the extreme. It is the dawn of the last day of training for the unit, and we are concentrating on the topic of mourning. Its course is different in the context of the AIDS epidemic. It does not correspond to the normal criteria. As in times of war, there is an urgency—no pause in which to weep and reach down into oneself. You have to be there for the people who are still alive and still fighting. But this does not mean that sadness is shelved. Memory and grief are constant—indeed, intensified by human interaction.

And there is so much grief in this group of volunteers. Anger, too. What about the baldness of funeral rites when all religious ceremony is denied? The interminable waiting in the crematorium, with the noise of the furnace and the equally terrible human silence. Not a word to recall the person one has accompanied, not a gesture that brings any meaning to the moment. Some people bitterly recall services that utterly ignored both the dying person's experience and that of his or her companions. Not a word about AIDS, not a word about the fight against the illness. Not a word of testimony to what the dying person may have brought to those who so lovingly shared the journey.

WHY NOT CREATE our own ritual of mourning? This morning before coming here, I went into a church and bought twenty little candles, the little red ones that burn in front of statues. Now we sit on the ground in a circle, all squeezed tightly together, because it's important to be able to feel the warmth of other human bodies. It is like being back at the beginning of the world, when men huddled around the only fire and told stories. The element of the primitive is healthy. Silence falls. Everyone is alert to one another, self-effacing. A woman lights the first candle, for Jean-Marc, she says. She talks about his courage and loneliness, which she tried to assuage as best she could. She would have liked to thank him before he died, but she didn't dare. She wants to talk to him now, in front of the group, and she's weeping quietly. Everyone lights a candle, one after the other, and the names string out like beads. There is an evident need to talk about those who've gone without a word being said. Words of gratitude, words of forgiveness sometimes, words of regret—the feelings come out quietly, discreetly, but they do come out. Sometimes someone starts to cry. The group remains calm. This provides a sense of security. It is possible to put one's grief into words, because it will be contained by the presence of the group.

ALL THE CANDLES are lit. Silence falls again, like a meditation or prayer, a silence full of thoughts honoring the memory and the lives of these young patients, now dead. One person begins spontaneously to sing; another recites a poem; another says a prayer. The ritual is over. Now it's time to separate again from those we've been remembering. Everyone in the group decides to take a deep breath and blow out the candles together. And as if to console themselves a little for this difficult gesture and to indicate that what has just been extinguished still burns in their hearts, they embrace one another freely, feeling how good it is to touch another body and know that one is alive.

◆

"DOES one die the way one has lived?" asks an old friend as we're having one of our regular dinners together at La Coupole. We're talking about our shared passion for the deeper regions of psychology and our ever-present curiosity about spiritual matters. I cherish the way we discuss our experiences and our viewpoints. His is totally original and free of any dogma. His clear perspective on things does me good. After a conversation with him, I often feel wiser, and as if my horizons had been expanded, too.

Does one die the way one has lived? My friend wants to know what I think. I have no answer. At the threshold of death, I have seen believers lose their faith and unbelievers discover faith for the first time.

Nobody is immune to moments of doubt and revolt, even when one has tried all one's life to come to terms with the idea of death. Contrariwise, there are some who live through a life of hell and who have a luminous death. Divine grace has nothing to do with merit.

As someone dying in Mother Teresa's care put it, "I will have lived the life of a beast, and I shall die like an angel."

The most beautiful death I ever witnessed was that of a young girl, a twenty-five-year-old drug addict with breast cancer that had spread. She had lived, in her own words, "a wild life." Her head was shaved and tattooed with the slogan "March or die." A loveless childhood, a hard, pointless life. Abandoned at birth by her prostitute mother, then taken in by her grandmother, she grew up like a wild plant, thirsty for love and the meaning of things, finding whatever she could to slake that thirst. As she said, she'd done it all. She was utterly without illusions. Her cancer came as hope of a kind: the hope that this dog's life would finally end. Drugs hadn't yet had time to destroy her.

If death were indeed to follow the image of the life that precedes it, one would have had to fear that this young girl would suffer hers in difficulty and torment, in revolt perhaps, or certainly in the greatest distress. Yet things turned out quite differently.

I tell my old friend how I found myself one morning at this girl's bedside. She was saying that she was going to die. The previous evening, she had asked her mother to bring a bottle of champagne, and they drank it together and talked about the good times they'd had, despite everything. It was her way of saying good-bye to this woman who had abandoned her but was still her mother.

And that morning, she had announced that she was going to die. Dr. Clement had asked me to go and see her. She was lying on her back, her head raised a little by the pillow. She had oxygen tubes in her nose; it seemed clear that her lungs were not functioning properly. There was a wet washcloth on her shaved forehead to bring down her fever. She was burning up, as I noticed when I took her hand.

She wanted to talk to me. But her voice was weak. I sat on a low stool so that I was at the height of her face and held my ear toward her lips. I could hear quite clearly that she was saying, "I'm going to die." Then she deliberately pulled out the plastic oxygen tubes and threw away the cloth that was drying on her forehead. As I stared at her, spellbound, she moved her body into the position women adopt for childbirth, legs spread. Her breath got shorter and noisier. But she seemed to be calm and not in pain.

For several minutes, I wondered whether I should reinsert the oxygen tubes, but her gesture had been so deliberate and she seemed at ease, so I decided to do nothing, but I stayed with her so that she wouldn't be alone. She said again, "I'm going to die." I began to stroke her forehead as she panted. She seemed to be pushing down on her legs, as if she were giving birth.

What came into my mind was Michel de M'Uzan's phrase about the spiritual labor that goes on inside every dying person: "an effort to give birth to oneself completely before leaving." Now for the first time, the expression corresponded to something absolutely real. This young woman, who had had such struggles with her life, was now birthing herself into a new world. I was filled with an emotion I cannot describe, part tenderness, part awe.

Her head slipped toward me a little. I lifted it gently and held it against me. At that moment, her breathing became blocked. Again I wanted to do something, reinsert the oxygen tubes. But I thought better of it. She was dying, as she had told me. Why should I disturb the simplicity and intimacy of this moment? She gasped in a mouthful of air, then stopped breathing again for several minutes. I murmured endearments to her that surfaced of themselves—from where, I have no idea. She could have been my daughter, and they were mother's words, which all mothers are born with, and which come to them from all eternity. A second time, she got her breath back. I had an image of a fish gasping on the sand. I wished I could put her back in the water. I wished I could give her life. There were tears in my eyes. It was the most intense moment I have ever experienced. She stopped breathing a third time, and the tension in her body suddenly gave way. I realized she had died.

My old friend is listening with tears in his eyes, too. We would both like to die with similar awareness and similar dignity.

◆

DEATH has been my daily companion for years, and I refuse to trivialize it. It has given me the most intense experiences of my life. I've known the pain of being separated from people I loved, the sense of impotence in the face of advancing illness, moments of revolt against the slow physical disintegration of people I was accompanying, and the temptation to put a stop to it all. I cannot deny the suffering and sometimes the horror that surround death. I've been witness to limitless solitude; I've felt the pain of being unable to share certain times of distress, because there are levels of despair so deep that they cannot be shared.

But alongside this suffering, I feel I have been enriched, that I've known moments of incomparable humanity and depth that I would not exchange for anything in the world, moments of joy and sweetness, incredible as that may seem. I know this is not unique to me, either.

SEVERAL years ago, I had the following dream. I was in the kitchen of an old house, with a man who seemed to be the host of this place. The man drew my attention to the wall above the fireplace. There was a hole in it. As he seemed to be insisting that I take a closer look, I got a chair, climbed up on it, and looked inside the chimney. I was astonished to discover that the inner surfaces coated in a thick layer of black soot were running with something that looked like honey. Intrigued, I put out my hand to test it—and it was honey!

I remember that in the dream, I was absolutely stunned by this discovery and I felt I simply must alert everyone else. It was as if I possessed a secret that must be shared as soon as possible. I knew they wouldn't want to believe me and that it would take time.

I KNOW there are lots of ways to interpret this dream, but when I had it, I associated it expressly with what I was discovering on a daily basis in my proximity to suffering and death. Yes, there was sadness, but there was also sweetness and often infinite tenderness. I was learning that the space-time continuum of death, for those who accept to enter it and see past the horror, is an unforgettable opportunity to experience true intimacy.

WRITING this has been my way of sharing this discovery.

A Note About the Author

MARIE DE HENNEZEL was born in France in 1946. She
started her career as a psychologist working with women
in distress and with cases of advanced psychosis. In 1987,
she joined the staff of the first palliative care unit in a Paris
hospital for people with terminal illnesses, where she
gathered the experiences she describes in this book. She
founded the Bernard Dutant Association—AIDS and Re-
Empowerment in 1990, in memory of a friend who died of
AIDS, and she gives lectures on approaching the end of life
and seminars on accompanying the dying. She lives in Paris
with her husband and three children.

A Note on the Type

PIERRE SIMON FOURNIER *le jeune*, who designed the type used in this book, was both an originator and a collector of types. His services to the art of printing were his design of letters, his creation of ornaments and initials, and his standardization of type sizes. His types are old style in character and sharply cut. In 1764 and 1766 he published his *Manuel typographique*, a treatise on the history of French types and printing, on typefounding in all its details, and on what many consider his most important contribution to typography—the measurement of type by the point system. In 1925 his type was revived by the Monotype Corporation of London.

Composed by ComCom, a division of Haddon Craftsmen, Allentown, Pennsylvania

Printed and Bound by R. R. Donnelley & Sons, Harrisonburg, Virginia

Designed by Misha Beletsky

DUE DATE			